Success Through Entrepreneurship
First Edition

DR. ALEX LABIAL SEÑARA

DR. ERIC P. LOZARITA

GREPPOO, INC

ABOUT THE AUTHOR

Alex Labial Señara, D.M

He is more exposed in business as he started his career at La Tondeña Distillers Incorporated in sales department as Salesman covering the area of Misamis Oriental and Bukidnon. He is also engaged in selling insurance product at PRULIFE U.K a London based insurance company. Aside from having an astounding experience in the industry, He is an academician by nature and has 18 years of teaching experience to include his current position as MBA and business professor of Aksum University, Ethiopia, Africa.

He was the Dean in the college of Commerce at Iligan Capitol College from 1999-2007, a Quality Assurance Manager of the Maritime Department of the Lyceum of Iligan Foundation. He handles the same position when he transferred to Southern Philippines College and added to his position as Quality Officer for Board Programs of the college. He also served as Internal Quality System Auditor and works towards the implementation of quality system imposed by external bodies like Norwegian and European International Organization for Standards, ISO. Active in different trainings and he is also a trainer on ISO, 5'S and other institutional requirements for certification and accreditations. He obtained his academic qualifications at Liceo de Cagayan University for his Bachelor of Science in Commerce major in management and economics. Finishes both his Master in Business Management and Doctor of Management at Capitol University.

Success through Entrepreneurship

Published by
Greppoo, Inc.
Davao City, Philippines

ISBN 978-1539981015

All rights reserved.
No part of this book may be
reproduced in any form or by any means
except brief quotations for a review or without
permission in writing from the publisher.

Cover design by

Pitros Pitiya

Edited by

Maria Lea Cecilia L. Bantilan

Printed by

Greppoo, Inc.
Davao City, Philippines

PREFACE

This introductory edition covers the basics of entrepreneurship activity and provides a complete overview for students and readers. The ideas, activities, projects and programs may aid the changing behaviour of the marketers and firms.

Entrepreneurship is an activity of creating an idea being put into reality through the efforts of imagination. It does not only apply the basic features of a created product but coming up with a real product that most consumers enjoy using them in their day-to-day existence. Thus, It is an art of defining projections into an actual tangible objects called goods and services offered in the market to satisfy human needs.

More so, it covers not only the transformation of an idea as well some activities which recognize opportunity like business. In line with it, business planning is a vital activity in defining and maintaining entrepreneurial growth. It considers as well a continuing research activity for effective forecasting and analysing possibilities to realize any business desire..

Further, it discusses the different concepts of entrepreneurial challenges using strategic approaches. Also, it uses a business model canvas as a tool for effective business practices as a guide to students, businessmen and other business enthusiasts.

Most importantly, a detailed activity involving procedural and developmental approaches are presented to enable students concretizes their creative ideas into reality. As a result, they will realize the value of a clear and well-defined product process presentation through exhibits and information drive which are beneficial for all users.

The Author

DEDICATION

To my ever loving wife, Doreen; my siblings: Ahleen Rose, Mary Aireen, Joseph Aries and Grandson A. J. Mathew Riley for their encouragement and support. To my mother-in-law, Merlits Hinacay Fabricante for her unending motivation and prayers. Without you, this book would have never been possible. Above all, to Almighty Lord Jesus, the source of life and wisdom.

Special thanks to Meseret Tsegay

-----Dr. Alex Labial Señara

TABLE OF CONTENTS

Chapter 1: **ENTREPRENEURSHIP: A FREE ENTERPRISE BUSINESS** 1
Introduction 1
The salient features of entrepreneurship 1
    Economic freedom 1
    Voluntary effort 2
    Private property 2
    Profit motive 2
Entrepreneurship defined 2
History of entrepreneurship 3
Characteristics of entrepreneurs 4
Important roles of an entrepreneur in the economy 6
Creativity and information- tool for entrepreneurs 8
What lies behind entrepreneurial success 10
Skills entrepreneurs need 12
Summary 14
Discussion questions 15
Key terms 16
Works cited 16

Chapter 2: **TRANSFORMING NEW BUSINESS IDEA THROUGH OPPORTUNITY RECOGNITION** 19
Introduction 19
Ways of recognizing opportunity 19
    What is Gap 19
    Opportunity 20
Techniques for generating ideas 21
Summary 23
Discussion questions 23
Key terms 23
Works cited 24

Chapter 3: **BUSINESS PLANNING** 25
Introduction 25
What is a business plan 25
Strategic importance of a business plan 26
    What is a SWOT analysis 26
Outlining the business plan 30

Ways of presenting a business plan 32
Summary 34
Discussion questions 35
Key terms 35
Works cited 36

Chapter 4: **THE PRODUCT CONCEPT** 38
Introduction 38
What is a product concept 38
Phases of product 42
Product protection 44
Product classifications 45
The product life cycle 46
Ways of extending product life 49
The role of price to product 51
Other ways to aid revenue generation for the firm 56
Summary 58
Discussion questions 59
Key terms 60
Works cited 60

Chapter 5: **MANAGING ENTREPRENEURIAL GROWTH** 63
Introduction 63
Importance of market positioning 63
The target market 65
The product brand 66
The 4 P's in marketing 68
Promotion 71
Summary 78
Discussion questions 79
Key terms 80
Works cited 80

Chapter 6: **DEVELOPING MARKET REASEARCH AND SALES FORECASTING** 83
Introduction 83
Doing the marketing research 83
The marketing research process 85
Sales forecasting 90
Techniques in forecasting 93

        Summary 95
        Discussion questions 98
        Key terms 98
        Works cited 98

Chapter 7: **THE INDUSTRY: Competitor Analysis and Social Responsibility** 100
        Introduction 100
        Industry analysis 101
        Economic trends 101
        Business trends 102
        Political trends 103
        Identifying Business Threats 103
        Product substitute 104
        Threat to new entrants 105
        Rivalry of the firm 108
        Supplier bargaining power 109
        Buyers bargaining power 110
        Analyzing competitor 111
        Summary 114
        Discussion questions 117
        Key terms 117
        Works cited 118
        Internet site addresses 118

Chapter 8: **PUTTING THINGS TOGETHER: Designing a Business of Your Own** 119
        Introduction 119
        Definition of terms 119
        The business and its applications 120
        The business environment 122
        Feasibility analysis and procedures 123
        Summary 128
        Discussion questions 131
        Key terms 132
        Works cited 132

Chapter 1

ENTREPRENEURSHIP: A FREE ENTERPRISE BUSINESS

Introduction

An entrepreneur is one who initiates to make money through the use of his skills with underlying risks. An Irish-French economist, Richard Cantillon described the term as anyone who is willing to launch a new venture or enterprise and must accept full responsibility for its outcome.

Entrepreneurs must have the ability to be resourceful in seeking opportunities and use resources to achieve goals like capital as one major resource. They must continue to search for opportunities and grab chances for their need to succeed. They also adopt a strong drive to control their future lives beyond satisfaction as they firmly believe that complete satisfaction can only be achieved through entrepreneurship ventures.

As time changes, the world is getting into a very complicated situation which creates an increasing awareness on how to go about entrepreneurship activity. People nowadays do not confine themselves to one business seeing lot of opportunities around. Entrepreneurs are said to be different sets of people. Aside from being creative, they see things which others fail to see. They often strive to create something new which brings some changes that will somehow help improve the economy through the creation of change, growth and advancements. Being unique and confident individuals, they are goal-oriented and strategic which are vital in a free enterprise economy where competition is very strong. Hence, they believe in the philosophy that using the right strategy makes the best man win.

THE SALIENT FEATURES OF ENTREPRENEURSHIP

This section presents the different features that embrace the activity of an entrepreneur ssuch as economic freedom, voluntary effort, private property, and profit in nature.

Economic freedom is giving the people the free exercise upon choosing the type of occupation they want to engage in. They have all the options whether to be in business or to work with someone. If they choose to venture into business, they are free to hire calibre and competent people and choose the most profitable product or services they want to produce.

Voluntary Effort is open to buyers and sellers who want to engage in the market transactions. The entry is free since no strong government intervention hinders anyone who is interested.

Private property is an opportunity that is given to people's right and privileges to make a personal control over their accumulated wealth and property for as long as they do not impede others' right.

Profit Motive is the driving force that motivates people to venture into business because of profit. When they try to engage in business, they think of profit in which by nature is one of the instruments that will improve people's lives and material well-being. They are willing to risk everything for such venture believing that their effort will give them the benefit and rewards they deserve.

ENTREPRENEURSHIP DEFINED

Entrepreneurship denotes different definitions that require better understanding for each reader.

Different definitions of the term entrepreneurship

- The activity of creating unlimited wealth by means of assuming risk in terms of investment, equity and time in providing for value for the rest of the stakeholders.
- It can also be defined as being creative, innovative in making something new of better value by using effectively the time, effort, capital and assuming risk to attain reward and satisfaction.
- It is an output of strong imagination from nothing. A process of creating something through an opportunity with the pursuance to succeed despite the risk factors.
- It is involved in building a long-term and sustainable cash flow streams. The major involvement lies in the creation and distribution of value benefit to different levels of consumers (individuals, group, organization and society).

> It is a human gift by being creative. Entrepreneurs have a clear vision, passion and commitment as their driving force to set and reach a goal.

THE HISTORY OF ENTREPRENEURSHIP

Its Features and Historical Perspective

> During the ancient period the word *entrepreneur* was used to refer to a person managing large commercial projects through the resources provided to him. In the 17th Century, this refers to a person who signed a contractual agreement with the government in order to provide stipulated products or to perform service In such case the contract price was fixed so any resulting profit or loss reflected the effort or performance of the entrepreneur.
> In the 18th Century the first theory of entrepreneur was developed by Richard Cantillon. He said that an entrepreneur is a risk taker. If we consider the merchant, farmers and /or the professionals they all operate at risk. For example, the merchants buy products at a known price and sell it at unknown price. It shows that they are operating at risk.
> Another development during the 18th Century was the differentiation of the entrepreneurial role from a capitalist role. The later role was the basis for today's venturing capitalist. In the late 19th and early 20th Century an entrepreneur viewed it from an economic perspective saying that an entrepreneur organizes and operates an enterprise for personal gain.
> In the middle of the 20th Century the notion of an entrepreneur as an inventor was established. "The function of the entrepreneur was to reform or revolutionize the pattern of production by exploiting an invention or discovering more generally untried technological possibilities for producing or reinventing new commodities or opening a new outlet for products by reorganizing a new industry."
> The concept of innovation and novelty is at the heart of the above definitions. Based on the historical development it is possible to understand the word *entrepreneur* which evolved from managing a commercial project to the application of innovation (creativity) through a business idea.

CHARCTERISTICS OF ENTREPRENEURS

To succeed in whatever endeavor one may engage in, he must exhibit certain incomparable characteristics upon deciding to pursue the challenge. Characteristics differ as to some degrees. Below are the qualities that fuel an entrepreneurial success:

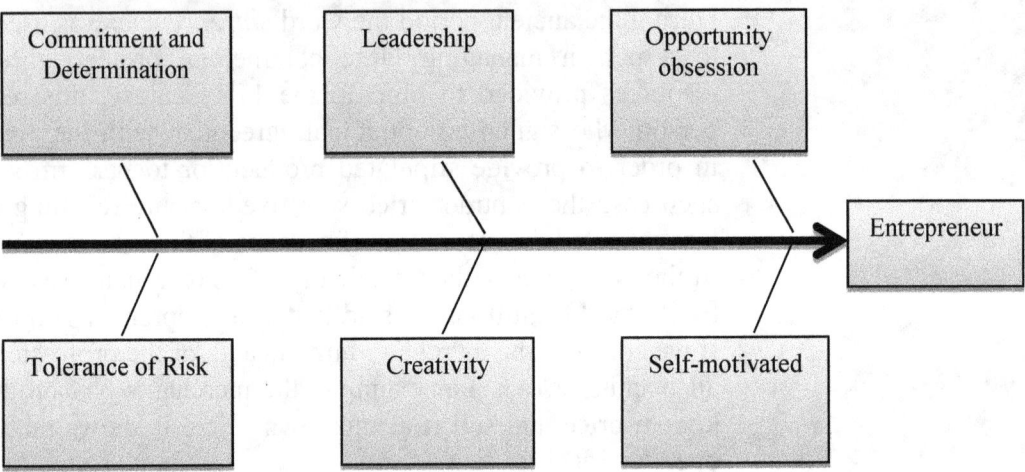

Figure 1 shows the different characteristics that embrace the activity of an entrepreneur.

Commitment and determination.

To be successful entrepreneurs, they must possess the behavior of being decisive, perseverant, well-disciplined, patient and will-powered to sacrifice and immerse themselves by heart at the right time to their business at all times.

Leadership.
They are team leaders, good listeners and coaches. A good leader will not set on his table rather practice the leadership by wandering around (MBWA) to ensure that everything is doing well.

Opportunity obsession.
They must be updated of the recent needs of their customers through valid sources and researches.

Tolerance of risk.
They must be problem-solvers to determine the root causes of any conflict and avoid any recurrence and handle risk properly.

Creativity
They must be flexible and open-minded to the changing needs of the environment. Fast learners must be prompt to address the business' needs.

Self-motivated
They are realistically goal- oriented people. They can work under pressure with a strong drive to achieve stated goals. They know how to convert their weaknesses into strengths and never lose focus on what they want to achieve.

Outlines of Successful Entrepreneurs

People whose qualities fit in the following areas can be potential entrepreneurs.

Characteristics	Description
Personal achievers	For an enterprise to grow, it requires great hard work. Self-motivated and independent-minded people can sacrifice personal desires against the business benefit.
Superior selling skills	Good social interactive skills enlist good listening, positive beliefs and creative minds. A successful business venture considers good rapport to customers as its main target for a long lasting business relationship.
Managerial skills	Being decisive, assertive and self-sacrificing merit a good manager to make any organization grow.
Skilled idea generator	They are dreamers who can transform ideas and innovations into a most desirable outcome.

Figure 2 outlines the description of successful entrepreneurs

IMPORTANT ROLES OF AN ENTREPRENEUR IN THE ECONOMY

Job creation is a potent contribution of an entrepreneur to the economy. He can provide solutions by creating wealth and improving the social standard of a country.

In Philippines, entrepreneurship is valued in empowering the poor, enhancing production and gearing towards innovation. The 1987 Philippine Constitution recognizes entrepreneurship as an engine of economic growth. It plays a vital role in supporting equitable income and wealth distribution, sustaining production of goods and services and expanding productivity and therefore, it improves the quality of life.

Another contribution of entrepreneurs to the economy is the effect of competitiveness among themselves which result to product innovation, market control and price moderation. They are challenged to create products of greater quality with affordable prices to meet the demands of the community. Whoever gives better services, better products and better prices merit customers' satisfaction.

On the other hand, according to Cornwall, it has been found out that 76 percent of business startups in 2003 were driven by the desire to pursue opportunities. This is an evidence that entrepreneurism is not a hindrance to the economy. Furthermore, it has been estimated that entrepreneurs have created 34 million new jobs since 1980 (Fox). Also, 70 percent of the new startups were already found to employ at least one person, and 80 percent still planned to hire within the next year (Cornwall). These data are significant proofs that entrepreneurism leads to creating new jobs; thus, it becomes a major contribution to the economy. Entrepreneurs also play a very important role in the aspect of maintaining and developing the economy of a nation. Some of their important economic activities are listed below:

1. Blending economic factors
2. Providing linkages
3. Accepting risk
4. Maximizing returns
5. Building Information

Blending economic factors

Before a product is introduced or released in the market, it has to undergo its processing. The product components include three major factors such as the raw materials, labor and capital. Then, the entrepreneurs combine them altogether and create a finished product as a means of satisfying human needs.

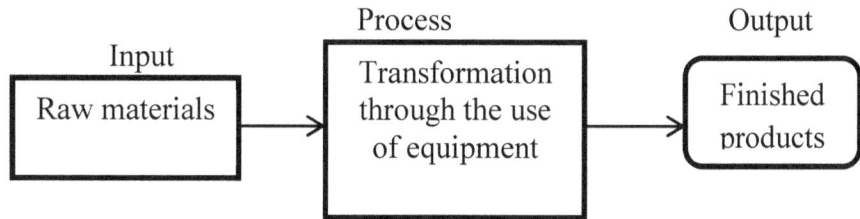

Figure 3 shows transformation process in blending the economic factors.

Providing linkages

The main objective of the entrepreneurs in creating the product is to satisfy human needs; however, this requires efficient means of distribution facilities to optimize desired benefits. Efficient distribution channels will help increase demand over and above profit and reduce the risk of competitors.

Accepting risk

Risk is turbulence in the attainment of the desired outcomes. These are business uncertainties where entrepreneurs are facing; hence, complete information is needed since no matter how they plan if there are always some unfavorable events that might come along the way, they hinder the possibility of realizing what they expect and hope for. Entrepreneurs as risk takers undermine the occurrence of these undesirable events for and in behalf of their concern about people and consumers as a whole.

Maximizing Returns

Good business invites some investors to expend their money as capital in a way will aid the entrepreneurs in meeting challenges on capital requirements and in return, provide them a favorable return in short and long terms.

Building Information

Entrepreneurs must be updated with the latest information about their business product. Through this generated information, they can make their product more competitive and sell it efficiently and create a reward through revenue. Recent updates enable them to embark on more opportunities.

CREATIVITY AND INFORMATION- TOOL FOR ENTREPRENEURS

In a competitive world, modern technologies play an important role in introducing products to the market where consumers are usually glued. Whether in print or broadcast, it calls and catches people's attention. Businessmen consider multi-media like radio, television, print or outdoor as effective channels of advertisement. The evolution of technology opens a new paradigm of investing on business. Any business idea can be borne through the widespread of modern technologies.

Innovation and invention compared

The terms differ from each other. Invention is a product of new discovery through the use of recent methods, materials and techniques. On the other hand, innovation is a process of modifying the existing one by making the quality better and giving a total satisfaction to users or consumers. More so, it contributes a favorable revenue generation to the entrepreneur. An inventor gives life to the innovator in the aspect of succession as the former serves as a source of their economic gain. Both parties can be done by one person to minimize expense but maximize profits. However, innovation requires more creativity than invention.

To note, creativity is a built-in ability of creating something new. It emphasizes on the "ability" rather than the "activity" itself of spreading something new to market existence.
Innovation is a process of modification from old to new things. The existing old product increases its value after it is converted anew and it becomes competitive bearing a new look, style, type or services. It is a process of transforming an old product using creative ideas; therefore, creativity is a product of innovation.

If creativity is an element that inspires an entrepreneur, innovation is the process of entrepreneurship. Below is a diagram showing the distinct relationship between invention and innovation.

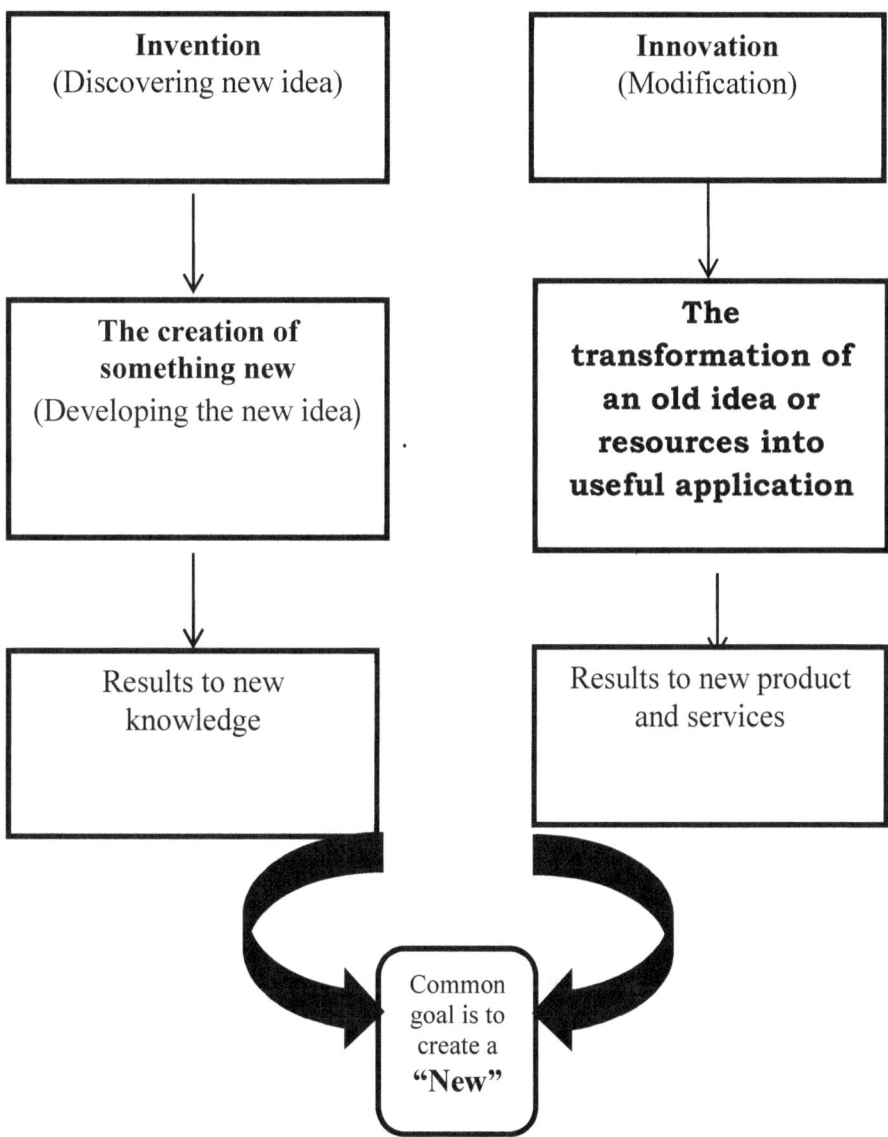

Figure 4 shows the different dimensions and approaches between invention and innovation.

Entrepreneur's strength

Some people ask whether entrepreneurs are born or made. Whatever it is, their most common virtue is strength. Below are the enumerated entrepreneurial strengths:
- Having the ability to innovate and bring significant changes and benefits to consumers.
- Being resourceful and having great innovative ideas to the society.
- Can contribute growth and progress.
- Can provide employment and generate income and wealth associated with successful innovation.
- Can create new technologies and products that displace the older ones.
- Risk takers who can make radical change.

The creativity process

In layman's understanding, most people believe that creativity is for those groups of selected and gifted people as they go through their ideas such as artist, scientist, composer and the like. Graham Wallas developed one of the early descriptions of creative process and is still very useful and widely used to guide creative process and come in four stages:
Preparation (the act of exploring and knowing the problem while seeing the opportunity behind in all directions)
Incubation (analyzing the problem or opportunity squarely)
Illumination (observing its brilliance of creativity effectiveness)
Verification (testing of the idea while reducing it to the most appropriate form and use).

The steps found in the process are very useful in the exploration of business problems. As such, the most common among other problems like losing your customers (what are the reasons? are we short of their expectations?) or this can be used as tool in identifying further opportunities of the business and for future product line creation.

WHAT LIES BEHIND THE ENTREPRENEURIAL SUCCESS?

It is always a prevailing challenge for many organizations on how to become successful in their quest for continuous improvement. Many organizations successfully move in vertical and horizontal direction as

they continue to grow during their business life cycle. Some of the contributing factors among others are the following:
1. Hard work
2. Market Demand for Product or Service Provided
3. Managerial Expertise
4. Luck
5. Strong Control System
6. Stable Capitalization

Hard work

Is an individual's strong desire to achieve goals. A hardworking person is motivated to perform their job beyond the minimum time. This shows a great deal of endurance and willingness to allocate long hours striving for a success in business. This strong desire to work briefly describes the nature of an entrepreneur.

Market Demand for Product or Service Provided

The business success greatly depends on the determination of sufficient demand for the product or services. Demand is the yardstick that motivates entrepreneur to produce such goods and services.

Managerial Expertise

Managing a business does not only require the basic knowledge on how to manage the business. He needs to apply his managerial expertise by seeing the possibilities that will help improve the business. The entrepreneur on the other hand must possess the so-called managerial competence.

Luck

Accordingly, some small businesses succeeded due to experiencing luck. Other successful entrepreneurs consider luck as a chance brought about by time. However, luck can happen if an entrepreneur possesses the principles of being ready for whatever unexpected opportunity to come.

Strong Control System

One of the entrepreneur's creeds is to have a strong control system in the different aspects of doing business. Business comprises different activities such as finance, manpower, inventory and the like that require a strong control over them for these will greatly affect the business operations.

Stable Capitalization

It is a common experience in small business on how to sustain and survive. However, there are many ways to increase capitalization and making them stable by using the resources wisely.

SKILLS ENTREPRENEURS NEED

Skills for many are viewed as outputs of experiences in different fields. These can add on the possibilities of making business a success if used effectively. A first time business venture could be difficult for some who do not have the skills but in the long run as they continuously gained experiences they become more flexible. Below summarize the different skills needed for a successful entrepreneur.

1. Resiliency
2. Focus
3. Invest in long-term
4. Find and manage people
5. Sell
6. Learn
7. Self-reflection
8. Self-reliance

Resiliency

It refers to an entrepreneur's ability to adapt and face whatever types of risks encountered in the course of doing business. He has the courage to control over unfavorable situations that the business experiences such as financial stress, threats, competition and the like.

Focus

It is an act by which the entrepreneurs' vigilance comes in when opportunity occurs. Observance is the key element in managing a company. An entrepreneur has to concentrate its resources to potential market rather than entering a narrow market without clear directions.

Invest in long-term

Long-term investment promises a favorable return than a short term. As time becomes uncertain, long-term investment could be more attractive (as the case of investing in the stock market). The amount invested in the long-term could be more diverse as business experts believe that the element of investment is time.

Find and manage people

Even how sophisticated the business is or in the case of large scale business with more capital intensive operations, people remain as the most effective resources. Successful entrepreneurs do not only keep within them their managerial skills to run business; however, a combination of both the managerial and human skills can be more effective in order to retain potential people to aid the achievement of the organizations' goal.

Sell

The heart and soul of every business operation is generating revenue and this can only be possible through selling. Selling can be done by anyone who wishes to make a sale; however, entrepreneurs should bear in mind that selling is not just an ordinary job. Some elements of effective selling are finding the right person with the right product, right time and a person who has the capacity and the decision to buy.

Learn

It is said that whatever you do on a day-to-day basis is a process of learning. Entrepreneurs do not only confine their understanding about their present business but they also need to know the external environment for a possibility of making business expansions in the future. Learning can be achieved by being active in participating in business organizations between business enthusiasts.

Self-reflection

It is the human capacity to do some exercises of meditation of what is going on in the business. It is a process of making a self-review on how the business is doing and a chance to make some innovative moves to further improve the business.

Self-reliance

It is a description of an entrepreneurial capability to stand alone as independent to what he/she is doing. Entrepreneurs are risk takers; hence, he can adjust to any success or failures.

SUMMARY

1. Entrepreneurship denotes different definitions; however, it was originally defined by an Irish-French economist, Richard Cantillon as anyone who is willing to launch a new venture or enterprise and accept full responsibility for the outcome.
2. Entrepreneurship employs the ability of being resourceful in seeking opportunities and uses resources with capital as its major resource to achieve goals. Entrepreneurs are deep thinkers who continue to search for opportunities and grab chances for their need to succeed. Entrepreneurship mentality adopts a strong drive by controlling future of their lives beyond satisfaction. They firmly believe that complete satisfaction can only be achieved through entrepreneurship ventures.
3. There are different salient features an entrepreneur possesses such as (1) economic freedom (2) voluntary effort (3) private property and (4) profit in nature.
4. Entrepreneurs succeed in their endeavour due to the passion of incomparable characteristics upon deciding to pursue the challenge. Their commitments are unquestioned more so with the determination to excel in business.
5. Entrepreneurs are regarded as unique individuals for they have the following characteristics such as (1) personal achiever (2) superior selling skills (3) managerial skills and (4) skilled idea generators.

6. The most important contribution of the entrepreneurs to the economy is creating more job opportunities. They also provide solutions by creating wealth and improve the social standard of the country.
7. Entrepreneurs play a very important role in the aspects of maintaining and developing the economy of a nation by (1) Blending the economic factors (2) Providing linkages (3) Accepting risks (4) maximizing returns and (5) building information.
8. Entrepreneurs are very creative in terms of introducing new venture in the market place and catching the attention of the prospect buyers. They are also innovative in making things more unique and differentiated by creating it something new.
9. They are types of people who love to assume risk and succeed in their quest for continued improvement and growth. Generally, they contributed a lot to the society using their strong imagination and creativity.
10. They have the skills such as (1) resilience (2) focus (3) invest in long-term (4) good in finding and managing people (5) sell (6) learn (7) self-reflection and (8) self-reliance.

DISCUSSION QUESTIONS

1. Why is entrepreneurship activity highly encouraged by the government and how does it help develop a society? Discuss.
2. How do entrepreneurs handle calculated risk in the conduct of creating a new venture? Discuss.
3. Are risk taking entrepreneurs born or made? Discuss.
4. Why is entrepreneurship activity called a free enterprise? Are there any obstacles to enter into this type of business?
5. Why are entrepreneurs required to do some self-reflections?
6. What are the different characteristics of an entrepreneur which are not present to those people who do not like to assume risk?

7. How important is valuing and managing people in the organization? Do good managerial skills assure people to perform? Discuss.
8. Entrepreneurs are known to be good in blending the economic factors. Is the act of doing considered as an art? Discuss.
9. Enumerate some of the entrepreneurial strengths that make them successful in their quest for making their business grow and contribute to the economic development?
10. Discuss the phrase, "Creating unlimited wealth by assuming risk'.

KEY TERMS (*in order of their appearance*)

entrepreneurs	*venture*	*launch*
risk		
economic freedom	*profit motive*	*innovative*
creativity		
historic perspective	*self-motivated*	*self-reflection*
blending		
job Creation	*economic factor*	*linkages*
invention		
optimization	*innovation*	*control system*
resiliency		

Works Cited

1. Benn, Piers. *Commitment*. Durham: Acumen, 2011. Print. Collier, Paul. *Breaking the Conflict Trap: Civil War and Development Policy*. Washington, DC: World Bank, 2003. Print.
2. Constant, Paule, Margot Miller, and France Grenaudier-Klijn. *Private Property*. Lincoln: U of Nebraska, 2011. Print.
3. Dai, Xiudian. *Innovation*. Singapore: World Scientific, 2015. Print.
4. Deida, David. *The Enlightened Sex Manual: Sexual Skills for the Superior Lover*. Boulder, CO: Sounds True, 2007. Print.
5. Greenberg, Herb, and Patrick Sweeney. *Succeed on Your Own Terms: Lessons from Top Achievers around the World on Developing Your Unique Potential*. New York: McGraw-Hill, 2006. Print.
6. Gupta, S. S. *Managerial Skills: Exploration in Practical Knowledge*. New Delhi: Global India Publications, 2008. Print.
7. Haan, Jakob De. *Economic Freedom*. Amsterdam: Elsevier, 2003. Print.

8. Hudson, Ken. *The Idea Generator: Tools for Business Growth*. Crows Nest, N.S.W.: Allen & Unwin, 2007. Print.
9. Johnson, Brett. *Lemon Leadership: Radically Fresh Leadership*. Cape Town: Struik Christian, 2012. Print.
10. Karataş-Özkan, Mine, and Elizabeth Chell. *Nascent Entrepreneurship and Learning*. Cheltenham, Glos, UK: Edward Elgar, 2010. Print.
11. Kim, Jeannie. *Creativity*. New York: Scholastic, 2002. Print.
12. Kirby, David A. *Entrepreneurship*. London: McGraw-Hill Education, 2003. Print.
13. Koehler, Gernot. *Job Creation: The Long-term Growth of Employment, Normal and Abnormal*. New York: Nova Science, 2008. Print.
14. Lam, Shui Fong. *Zen Yang Jiao Hai Zi Zi Dong Zi Jue*. Xianggang: Cheng Zhang Zong He Fu Wu Zhong Xin, 2002. Print.
15. *Linkages: Manufacturing Trends in Electronics Interconnection Technology*. Washington, D.C.: National Academies, 2005. Print.
16. Lucarelli, Caterina, and Gianni Brighetti. *Risk Tolerance in Financial Decision Making*. Houndmills, Basingstoke, Hampshire: Palgrave Macmillan, 2011. Print.
17. Marcinko, David E. *Business of Medical Practice: Advanced Profit Maximization Techniques for Savvy Doctors*. New York, NY: Springer Pub., 2004. Print.
18. Milanović, Petar T. *Water Resources Engineering in Karst*. Boca Raton, FL: CRC, 2004. Print.
19. Murphy, Warren. *Profit Motive*. Place of Publication Not Identified: E-Rights E-Reads, 2008. Print.
20. Sadler, Philip. *Leadership*. London: Kogan Page, 2003. Print.
21. Tate, Natasha. *An Inconvenient Obsession*. Toronto: Harlequin, 2011. Print.
22. Benn, Piers. Commitment. Durham: Acumen, 2011. Print.
23. Collier, Paul. Breaking the Conflict Trap: Civil War and Development Policy. Washington, DC: World Bank, 2003. Print.
24. Constant, Paule, Margot Miller, and France Grenaudier-Klijn. Private Property. Lincoln: U of Nebraska, 2011. Print.
25. Dai, Xiudian. Innovation. Singapore: World Scientific, 2015. Print.
26. Deida, David. The Enlightened Sex Manual: Sexual Skills for the Superior Lover. Boulder, CO: Sounds True, 2007. Print.
27. Greenberg, Herb, and Patrick Sweeney. Succeed on Your Own Terms: Lessons from Top Achievers around the World on

Developing Your Unique Potential. New York: McGraw-Hill, 2006. Print.
28. Gupta, S. S. Managerial Skills: Exploration in Practical Knowledge. New Delhi: Global India Publications, 2008. Print.
29. Haan, Jakob De. Economic Freedom. Amsterdam: Elsevier, 2003. Print.
30. Hudson, Ken. The Idea Generator: Tools for Business Growth. Crows Nest, N.S.W.: Allen & Unwin, 2007. Print.
31. Johnson, Brett. Lemon Leadership: Radically Fresh Leadership. Cape Town: Struik Christian, 2012. Print.
32. Karataş-Özkan, Mine, and Elizabeth Chell. Nascent Entrepreneurship and Learning. Cheltenham, Glos, UK: Edward Elgar, 2010. Print.
33. Kim, Jeannie. Creativity. New York: Scholastic, 2002. Print.
34. Kirby, David A. Entrepreneurship. London: McGraw-Hill Education, 2003. Print.
35. Koehler, Gernot. Job Creation: The Long-term Growth of Employment, Normal and Abnormal. New York: Nova Science, 2008. Print.
36. Lam, Shui Fong. Zen Yang Jiao Hai Zi Zi Dong Zi Jue. Xianggang: Cheng Zhang Zong He Fu Wu Zhong Xin, 2002. Print.
37. Linkages: Manufacturing Trends in Electronics Interconnection Technology. Washington, D.C.: National Academies, 2005. Print.
38. Lucarelli, Caterina, and Gianni Brighetti. Risk Tolerance in Financial Decision Making. Houndmills, Basingstoke, Hampshire: Palgrave Macmillan, 2011. Print.
39. Marcinko, David E. Business of Medical Practice: Advanced Profit Maximization Techniques for Savvy Doctors. New York, NY: Springer Pub., 2004. Print.
40. Milanović, Petar T. Water Resources Engineering in Karst. Boca Raton, FL: CRC, 2004. Print.
41. Murphy, Warren. Profit Motive. Place of Publication Not Identified: E-Rights E-Reads, 2008. Print.
42. Sadler, Philip. Leadership. London: Kogan Page, 2003. Print.
43. Tate, Natasha. An Inconvenient Obsession. Toronto: Harlequin, 2011. Print.

INTERNET SITE ADDRESSES

1. For the list of major skills for every entrepreneurs, see: http://www.forbes.com/sites/aileron/2013/11/26

Chapter 2

TRANSFORMING NEW BUSINESS IDEA THROUGH OPPORTUNITY RECOGNITION

Introduction

One of the skills the entrepreneurs possess is the ability to recognize opportunity which serves as their initial capital towards the development of a new product venture.

As discussed in Chapter 1, a free enterprise is a business nature that is embraced by a strong market competition. Different business players surround the market making it difficult for an entrepreneur to succeed in his endeavour specifically when he/she fails to recognize some opportunities within the business environment. To sustain in the business, one must be vigilant in searching for a new business idea considering that the entire product is not exempted to experience the product life cycle. A continuous search for new business idea will help entrepreneurs to continue producing new product that will delight customer's desires. The evolution of technology nowadays is very tremendous; new product introduced in the market has a very limited life due to increasing number of new products available in the market; thus, more new ideas are needed to fill in the wants of the existing customers.

WAYS OF RECOGNIZING OPPORTUNITY

More seasoned entrepreneurs will always say that opportunity is just around the corner; however, for some who don't have the capacity of recognizing them find it the other way. A sales person always considers opportunity as an occurrence which involves time, occasion, moment or any set of favorable circumstances. In business, the general principles of identifying opportunity come when there is a presence of "gap" in anything.

What is Gap?

The term denotes between supply and demand. Both of these factors are favorable on the part of the entrepreneurs for these are motivators for them to start creating and innovating for something to fill in a gap. Gap generally is defined as the inability of suppliers to provide the quantity demanded by customers (more demand than supply or vice versa).

Sometimes information regarding the gap is crucial to entrepreneurs if they will react immediately on the given information. Before reacting to the predetermined gap, entrepreneurs must initiate to:

1. identify the consumers' need,
2. know their willingness to buy so that the entrepreneurs can design a product appropriate to the need of the target customers. An illustration is given to create a more comprehensive understanding about gap.

Table showing the gap of selected products			
Product description	Quantity demanded (. In '000 units)	Quantity Supplied (In '000 units)	Gap (In '000 units.)
Refrigerator	350	200	150
Car	150	60	90
Emergency light	250	120	130
Computer	1500	1200	300
Cellular phones	20,000	10,000	10,000
Laptop	25,000	15,000	10,000
Power bank	3,000	900	2,100

Figure 2 shows the relationship between supply versus demand that creates a gap

From the above information reflected in the table, entrepreneurs can now make a necessary decision to purse their desire to create new product because the gap is convincingly favorable. There is certainty that whatever product or services created and innovated by them will assure investment worth.

Opportunity

Is an unexpected favorable event that permits entrepreneurs to do something. An opportunity has four major elements that are essential to every product or services where entrepreneurs take advantage in creating valuable product for their buyers or users.

1. It should be attractive.
2. It should be robust.
3. It should be timely.
4. It should be anchored to the product.

It should be attractive.

Attractiveness does not compromise; however, it is a must for entrepreneurs to have a very attractive opportunity for this will increase their confidence in the realization of their created new venture. Attractive opportunity defines clearly the degree of success of the proposed venture considering that all the positive elements are present.

It should be robust.

It should be robust enough to sustain the opportunity. There are opportunities which are classified as temporary in nature. They create chaos to entrepreneurs considering that opportunity triggers them to make an out-of-pocket investment to finance the project; hence, verification as to its sustainability is needed.

It should be timely.

Successful entrepreneurs always consider time as the number one element of success as what people said time is gold. The multiple of earnings is measured by time hence; a true and clear opportunity should be timely. The introduction of modern and sophisticated gadgets like cell phones is said to be timely. The term timely in business refers to the presence of astounding demand and backed by consumer's degree of willingness to buy.

It should be anchored to the product.

Product is the tangible element intended for sale to end users. Opportunity is said to be favorable if the product carries a very effective design that delights customers. Product must contain a promise of satisfying the end users hence, quality and quantity need not be sacrificed.

TECHNIQUES FOR GENERATING IDEAS

Most of the time entrepreneurs meet and talk together and share different experiences as they go through and face day-to-day challenges. Generally, as a result of exchange of ideas, they will be able to generate more ideas than opportunity. Spotted good ideas will be capitalized as opportunity. Some of these approaches can be viewed as brainstorming and focus group.

Brainstorming

Is the process of grouping different levels of entrepreneurial understanding to discuss potential ideas. It is done on one venue wherein every participant collects ideas and records it for further assessment.

In the actual setting, the brainstorming activity is interactive where every member shares his/her experiences to others. One might present his/her idea and others might do some comments and verification of one's opinion. The brainstorming process requires some specific procedures shown below as guidance of the said activity.

Procedures in conducting a Formal Brainstorming

Rule	Explanation
1	No criticism is allowed, including chuckles, raise every eyebrows, or facial expressions that express skeptisms or doubt. Criticism stymies creativity and inhibits the free flow of ideas.
2	Freewheeling is the care free expression of ideas free from rules or restraint; thus, it is encouraged; the more ideas, the better. Every crazy or outlandish idea may lead to a good idea or a solution to a problem.
3	The session moves quickly, and nothing is permitted to slow down its pace. For example, it is more important to capture the essence of the idea than to take the time to write down neatly.
4	Leapfrogging is encouraged. This means that the idea is carried over to form another new.

Figure 2 shows the elements of conducting a formal brainstorming. Source: Bruce R. Barringer and R. Duane Ireland, fourth edition: entrepreneurship "Successfully Launching New Ventures"

Focus group

This kind of approach can be applicable in different fields such as conducting survey, research and the like for the purposes of determining the best idea. Political activity also applies these techniques by asking people such as, who is their potential choice for the position. Some also group potential people in one area and discuss things related to the purpose.

The focus group in general is a process of selecting potential participants (not more than 10) because they are the potential people that can defend issues being discussed. For a clearer understanding about how to go about conducting a focus group, below summarizes some elements needed:
- Determine the members
- Formulate focus group questions
- Prepare the participants
- Implement the interview
- Analyse result

SUMMARY

1. Business idea is a very important factor that leads entrepreneurs in the transformation process. Recognition of opportunity is very vital; however, sometimes it is crucial to them the moment they fail to recognize the basic elements for them to decide to venture on it such as the willingness to buy and the kind of product customers need.
2. There are ways that help the entrepreneurs to make finality of their decision such as finding the gap between supply and demand. Gap is the essential factor for it is the yardstick that assures the potential investment return made by entrepreneurs.
3. Opportunity as depicted by most of the entrepreneurs is viewed as unexpected favorable outcomes that permit them to do something of value and it consists of different elements that will delight customers.
4. Different techniques that are applicable in creating ideas can be done through brainstorming and focus group activity. These are potential activity that will lead entrepreneurs realize the idea in mind through the shared information from different levels of respondents; however, all the procedures are governed with strict guidelines for purposes of attaining the ultimate goal.

DISCUSSION QUESTIONS

1. Why is idea recognition important to every entrepreneur? Does failure for them to generate idea hinder him to launch a new venture? Discuss.
2. Opportunity is just around the corner as they said. Give at least one element that aids entrepreneurs on recognizing opportunity.
3. If gap is applicable between supply and demand, how important is it to them (entrepreneurs) in decision making? Discuss.
4. Does attractive opportunity promise a favorable investment return? If so, discuss.
5. How does brainstorming differ from focus group? Enumerate some of the similarities and differences?

KEY YERMS *(in order of their appearance)*

Skills	entrepreneurs	opportunity	product
venture supply	demand		predetermined gap

Investment worth   **attractive opportunity**   **customer delight brainstorming**
focus group   **idea generation**

Works Cited

1. Amadeu, and Abel Carrasco. *Brainstorming*. Genève: Paquet, 2002. Print.
2. Corrao, Sabrina. *Il Focus Group*. Milano: Angeli, 2000. Print.
3. Grimshaw, Charlotte. *Opportunity*. Auckland, N.Z.: Vintage, 2007. Print.
4. Hougaard, Søren. *The Business Idea: The Early Stages of Entrepreneurship*. Berlin: Springer, 2005. Print.
5. Hougaard, Søren. *The Business Idea: The Early Stages of Entrepreneurship*. Berlin: Springer, 2005. Print.
6. Kotler, Philip, and Gary Armstrong. *Principles of Marketing*. Boston: Pearson Prentice Hall, 2012. Print.
7. Trigiani, Adriana. *Home to Big Stone Gap: A Novel*. New York: Random House, 2006. Print.
8. P.J Murphy. Conceptual Foundation of entrepreneurial Discovery Theory; entrepreneurship theory, Prentice Hall, 2010.
9. J.M. Haynie, D. Shepherd." A Situated Metacognitive Model of the Entrepreneurial Mind set, Prentice Hall, 2010.
10. K. Rodan, "Entrepreneurial Thoughts, Stanford Technology Program, 2011.
11. Carrion, Juan Antonio "Entrepreneurial Imperatives" GIC Enterprises and Co., Inc., 1990

INTERNET SITE ADDRESSES

1. *For the list of definition of opportunity, see: https://www.google.com.et/search*

Chapter 3

BUSINESS PLANNING

Introduction

The popular word of Benjamin Franklin says that "if you fail to plan you are planning to fail". Successful businessmen must make a plan prior to initiate any move. To plan is the first and crucial step for any business start-up. It lays down well-defined procedures that project how the business will function. A plan can be viewed in many ways depending on what venture one may engage in. As such, if a person engages in sport he will prepare a game plan. Likewise a combatant prior to get into the field where enemy is situated prepares a tactical plan. In the case of a business plan, variety of requirements needed involving all major components like monetary, man power for production and their proceedings are based on business feasibility study. The activity is crucial in running the business; therefore, planning must be made clear and well-defined for it will foresee all possible opportunities and threats, determine the existing demands and match all these factors against the resources needed in order to succeed in the business. Thus, successful business enthusiasts believe that a good plan is half done.

WHAT IS A BUSINESS PLAN?

Definition

Generally, the term business plan *is a document that describes a clear detailed proposed venture* which leads any business activity towards getting the desired goals. It focuses on identifying the target market, finding ways to capture them and making use of the advantages that the firm has. It strategizes countering business competition and also qualifies the skilled and capable players to man the business. Business plan also determines the different strategies to be used and implemented.

The business plan and its purpose as stated earlier, there are various types of plan whose application matters most according to its use; however, the main purpose is to guide strategically in the development of the business venture. A good plan illustrates the current status of the environment, expected needs, and projects results. Its main trust is to create a very strategic and comprehensive design for the external parties to understand the business concept. Below enumerate some major purposes of the plan.

It provides guidance for entrepreneurs in designing a well-defined and logical structure upon implementing its management strategies to realize its time frame. It can be a financial source. A well-defined business plan can be used for negotiation to identify financial institutions offering loans or capital investment. and can be used as a point of reference to benchmark potential improvement and measure its effectiveness in the course of its implementation.

STRATEGIC IMPORTANCE OF BUSINESS PLAN

A plan is very important because it will make or break the future of the business. As an entrepreneur, he must be aware of its different aspects where the projected result lies largely on its effective implementation. Planning seems very technical by nature; hence, a good plan must be guided by a SWOT analysis.

What is a SWOT analysis?

It is an organization's initiative that points out how strong the firm is in terms of possessing their internal strength and weaknesses including opportunities and threats as it referential advantages.

The elements of SWOT are classified into two categories:
1. Internal (the strengths and weaknesses)
2. External (the opportunities and threats)

Strengths. They serve as the company's internal factors. These elements can be capitalized by the entrepreneurs in making their venture strong enough, creating product dominance and expecting larger market share as much as possible..

Weaknesses. These are the unfavorable conditions affecting company's long-term goals if not addressed properly.

Opportunities. They are external in nature where the entrepreneurs must look up to. These are favorable events that an entrepreneur must take into account. Most experts say that opportunities are just around and recognizing them is very important.

Threat. It is an element that affects the business operations which can either be natural or artificial. A natural threat is brought about by nature; however, an artificial threat is created by human being to their advantage.

The SWOT analysis can affect the business in different ways depending on how appropriate entrepreneurs utilize them; thus, technical application is required. The effects of SWOT if not properly used are shown below.

Company "A"   Company "B"

Strengths 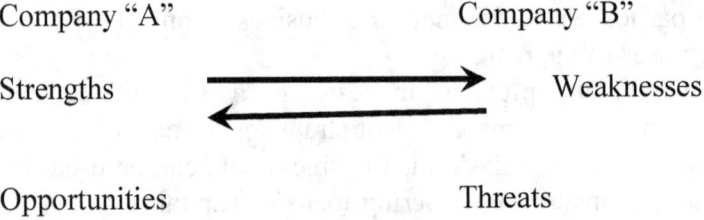 Weaknesses

Opportunities   Threats

Figure 1 shows the effects of the SWOT factor if not used by entrepreneurs to their advantage.

Company A's strengths can turn out into their own weaknesses if they will not keep themselves firm in their position such as keeping their product dominant in the market. Competitors always look at the weak side of the firm and take advantage of it. George, a sales man dominated the product in the market for a long time. His strong product dominance was his strength. He had no problem in delivering sales requirements in the company because his performance exhibits very exemplary. However, his strength slowly became a weakness because he could no longer attend to other customers because of the strong demand of big dealers making the other outlets experienced stock outs. It became an opportunity for the competitors seeing the situation to capitalize on George's lapses and succeed in capturing a portion of its market dominance. As years went by and as competitors began to create a market of their own, the product dominance of George began to decline and eventually the situation turned out the other way around. Being over confident of keeping one's strength sometime brings some crucial impact; hence, all the elements found in the SWOT create a vice-versa effect.

Company "A"   Company "B"

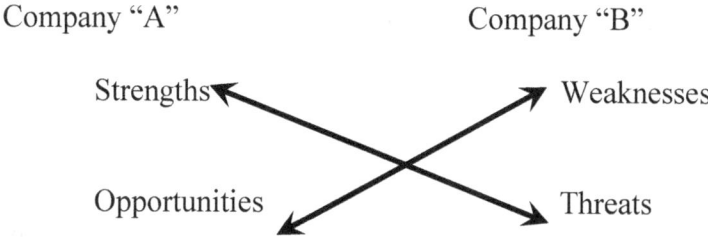

Figure 2 shows the inverse impact on the element of SWOT if not used appropriately.

Ways of identifying the elements of SWOT analysis (Product based)

Internal	External
Strengths Excellent sales force Strong customer relationship Excellent internal communication system Excellent location	**Weaknesses** delayed delivery High inventory levels Inefficient recording system Poor market research Unstable financial capacity
Opportunities High demand of product Having loyal customers Similar product with poor quality Seasonal high demand	**Threats** Plenty of competitors Competitors launch new advertising Unfavorable economy New entrants coming into the market.

How to go about achieving SWOT analysis

SWOT analysis is a process of collecting all potential operational problems that will affect the organization towards their set goals. It is very essential to all types of business be it stable or not. Below summarize the steps towards achieving SWOT activity.

- ➤ Strategic planning
- ➤ Determining potential problems
- ➤ Collating/prioritizing

Strategic planning

It is an organizational activity that defines priorities among the many and focuses the resources needed to strengthen its operations and by ensuring all elements conform to the common goals. A strategic activity is also an instrument that identifies the organization's weaknesses and converts them into strengths. The activities involve asking all the participants regarding their observations which will somehow become a problem to the operation.

Determining potential problems

All business activities embrace different problems. In spite of their numerous challenges, an entrepreneur must be able to recognize them with their degree of importance and their impact to the business.

Collate problems

Collating is a process of defining and segregating the enumerated problems according to their degree of importance. They should be categorized as to annual and long-term like 2-5 years. After collating the problems, the top management can readily answer the problems strategically. Below illustrates the strategic planning activity.

Summary of problems

> Lack of knowledge, poor customer relations, low profit return, no enough budget, poor management skills, incompetent technology, strong competition, many identical products, poor distribution facilities, lack of product awareness.

The collated problems above must be arranged according to their degree of urgency so that the management can act accordingly and addresses the problems by matching the resources needed. Below identifies nature of the collated problems.

Degree of action needed

Urgent	**short term**	**Long-term**
-Lack of knowledge technology	- no enough budget	incompetent
-Poor customer relation facility	-poor management skills	poor distribution
- Low profit return	- strong competition	
- Many identical products		
- Lack of product awareness		

The enumerated problems are now classified according to their degree of need. These must be contained in the strategic plan so that possible solutions can be drawn and analyzed by their effectiveness in answering the perceived difficulties.

Sample development plan with template (Urgent plan)

Problem Area	Current Status	Objectives	Strategy	Person(s) involve	Time frame & budget	Remarks

Figure 4 shows the template of the development plan as a guide to strategic planning

OUTLINING THE BUSINESS PLAN

All business plans have identical contentions; however, they will vary according to the desire of the founders of the business. Below suggests an outline for the business plan.

Executive Summary

It is a short overview of the whole business plan. It provides the readers the information they need about the new venture and assess what is distinct in it. It should be written in an interesting manner to attract interested party to read the content of the plan.

Description of the business

This section contains a more comprehensive component of the venture. The description of the business suggests being short but comprehensive that details the company's history and incorporates therein the industry itself. The product and services should be described in such a way the readers will be able to determine its uniqueness and goals and clarify specific milestones.

Marketing Analysis

Marketing is the heart of every business venture; hence, it must be defined clearly. Target market must be identified such as the potential buyers of the product to whom services are also rendered. Market size is also a very important element so entrepreneurs can benchmark production volume over and above the existing competition. Another important element that adds on color to a marketing plan is how to market the product itself. The specifics about the strategies used, methods of distribution, pricing, choices of advertising and the like reflect the beauty of the plan.

The Research, Design and Development (R&D)

The product must be upgraded or enhanced in order to cater the changing needs of the customers. This can be possible through research. Creating a research and development department is a challenge faced by most of the entrepreneurs considering budget allocation. Although budget requirement for this endeavor is somewhat big enough but successful business undermines this because research helps in many ways such as providing information as to the time for innovation and protecting the product to experience from obsolescence.

Location

This section needs careful analysis in deciding where to establish the new business venture. Location is always critical on the part of the investors considering that there are lots of factors to be kept in mind. Some of the factors to consider are the following:

Proximity to suppliers of raw materials. Location of the business when situated closer to the supplier of raw materials can be an advantage to them with their product rates. The favorable pricing for any commodity brings a considerable strength to the firm for they can use this as a marketing tool to induce buyers to buy their products rather than those from the competitors,

Availability of transportation. Distribution is always a challenge faced by entrepreneurs in their day-to-day activity. Accessible transportation benefits the manufacturers for this will not require them to use their own resources to distribute goods to target customers. Customers can readily purchase their needs because of the presence of transportation.

Cost of labor. Labor intensive industry needs more manpower in the production process. Labor is a variable; hence, cost of labor shares huge operational expenses that affect the revenue generation of the firm and the investors. Some international firms expand business operations to places where the cost of labor is less in order to generate a reasonable return of their investment. They consider variable cost as crucial in the operation like fixed facilities which they can determine in advance.

Management The success of any venture lies largely to somebody who represents the management team. Business is set to be long-term in nature; hence, the management should be aware on how to keep potential people. Keeping potential people dictates management to incorporate some methods of compensation for them to be energetic. Employing other non-monetary or extrinsic motivation with value is necessary to create an atmosphere of comfort while productivity increases.

Critical risks Risk is everywhere; however, the beauty of it is they are controllable. A good planning scheme will address the occurrence of risk; hence, it must be analyzed carefully to uncover them before they arise. Management might decide to hire some consultants purposely to aid them in making a smooth business venture.

Financial forecasting. Financial forecasting is the major element that assures the success of every business ventures. Budgeting is the key. Forecasting methods help the firm in achieving leverage such as having enough inventories for sale.

The activity entails monitoring every aspect of the business and all potential expenses incurred should undergo right forecasting. It also provides a standard measure to determine the possible outcome of the operation. Thus, financial projection will serve as a tool for the management in controlling the business as it prospers to the next level.

Landmark Schedule. This segment of a business plan defines the objectives and the forecasted time of its accomplishments. Set goals and time frame requires a thorough review in order to know the elements that contribute in the realization of the predetermined objectives. It is necessary and true to whatever things one must do considering that every activity for that matter needs to be reviewed to benchmark possibilities of improvements and for future development plan management should do.

Appendix. The last part of the business plan yet the most important one serves as the reference to which the valued information are taken or cited. The term itself denotes that other materials which supplement the business plan are reflected here such as agreement, tag lines, name of advisers, bibliography to make the plan more reliable and well-documented.

WAYS OF PRESENTING A BUSINESS PLAN

During the start of designing a business plan, the sole intention is to make it more comprehensive in order to attract investors and to possibility source out finances from banks and other government entities. After its completion, the next step is to market the business plan in order to identify the investors personally. Most often than not, investors really want to see the founders of the venture to see some favorable impressions of the business. The ultimate way of presenting the business plan can be through personal or the use of power point in the case of a classroom type presentation.

The Personal Oral Presentation of the Plan (PLEASE CHECK BOLD TERMS. The presentation process of the business plan is aimed at convincing potential investors to set aside a portion of their available resources such as financial and tangible financial vehicles. Expected contents in the presentation involve:
- The goal of the venture,
- Benefits to the society as a whole
- The ROI,
- Expansion plan.

The goal of the venture

A clear goal derived from a good business plan entices investor to invest in the new venture; hence, goals of the business should clearly promise a favorable investment return.

Benefits to the society as a whole

Creating a new venture does not only benefit the founder of the venture but the society as well. It cannot be denied that creating a new venture brings forth a domino effect to the life of the people through employment. The generated earnings from employment empower their purchasing power which gives life to small business. In general, the new business venture makes the economic system evolves productively.

The ROI

This portion of the business plan is considered as the most critical on the part of the investors. Since they (the investors) put an amount of money for the business, they are also sensitive on their return of investment. Time is the essence of any form of investment; hence, the shorter the time involved in giving the ROI indicates that the business is doing well.

The expansion plan

A business plan presentation does not only limit in summarizing the possibility of earning for investors, benefits contributed to the society and other businesses alike, it also covers the future business expansion. Future plan is very essential considering that it is a long-term venture; thus, it is important to include some details on how to go about expanding business locally or internationally.

The presenter of the business plan should expect some questions that may arise in the course of the presentation either from the investors, stakeholders and the society. Below enumerate some potential questions a presenter must answer:

> *Is the business just an idea, or is it an opportunity with real potential?*
> *Is the product or service viable? Does it give significant value to the customers? Has a feasibility analysis been completed? If so, what are the results?*
> *Is the business entering an exciting, growing industry with an attractive position within?*
> *Does the business have a well-defined target market?*
> *Does the business have points of differentiation that truly separate itself from its competitors? Are these points of differentiation sustainable?*
> *Does the business have a sound marketing plan?*
> *Is the management team experienced, skilled, and prepared to the task of launching the new firm?*
> *Is the business' operation plan appropriate and sound?*
> *Are the firm's financial projections realistic based on assumptions?*
> *Are the financial projections completed correctly as they project a bright future for the firm?*

Figure 5 shows ten most important questions in the business plan. Source: Bruce R. Barringerm R. Duane Ireland; Entrepreneurship, Successfully Launching New venture. Pp 159

SUMMARY

A business plan is very important to whatever endeavor for it contributes to the success in any new venture. It helps the society as a whole by providing employment to people, creating more business opportunities like increasing the purchasing power of the consumers.

A plan is generally a written document that describes how the business looks like by giving a complete detail of the proposed venture. It encourages potential investors who are interested about the business. A good plan summarizes different strategies the business will use to ensure the realization of their goals.

A plan maybe identical or may vary depending on the understanding of the founders. It should illustrate the total status of the environment in order to understand the need of the targeted consumers. A good plan must guide the entrepreneurs find solutions to their financial needs.

It should be strategic in order to ensure the effective ways of achieving goals. The use of strategic approach in planning is very useful to entrepreneurs considering that the activity is tantamount in attaining its goals. The strategic approach in solving problem employs the use of SWOT analysis to create a clear direction and find effective ways of solving problems.

The SWOT helps the entrepreneurs determine different strength, weaknesses, opportunities, and weaknesses that affect the business operations. This will also guide ventures on how to capitalize its component to their advantage. The use of SWOT analysis is not only helping the firm to predict and address its business problems but it is also a useful tool to improve its performance in the market. This kind of strategy helps the firm owners in terms of addressing problems through advance information.

Every business is not exempted to experience any problem; however, knowing its individual strengths and weaknesses enables the firm to capitalize from them for its improvement in the right place and time. It is suggested therefore that the firm should know how to use those elements considering that strengths and weaknesses are favorable to entrepreneurs but they may serve as threats as well if not properly utilized.

Success in business largely depends on the readiness of the founder. Business planning is the only tool that will aid entrepreneurs to achieve their goals in a very easy way.

Knowledge in making a business plan is very important to any type of business. Every component necessitates the readers to understand so their interest may set upon the business. Hence, a plan should be structured well, articulated and realistic. The element of business planning is the presentation itself to potential investors, financial institutions and other third parties of interest. It requires a full knowledge of the plan considering that during the presentation, questions, verifications and clarification will surely arise. The role of the presenter is so crucial because he presents the overall package of the plan; thus, he must be knowledgeable enough to convince the investors and financial institutions to consider the business plan.

DISCUSSION QUESTIONS

1. Why must we plan? According to business experts planning leads to business success. Why do some businesses fail despite the presence of a good plan? Discuss.

2. Why does a business plan need to be written? What are the essential parts of doing it? Discuss.
3. Discuss the elements of SWOT analysis. What are the advantages of the components to the firm? When can these be drawn to the entrepreneur's disadvantage?
4. Why do some business firms find difficulty in determining their weaknesses?
5. Discuss the important elements of strategic planning and how to get started with the activity?
6. What are the potential business problems? In what way can entrepreneurs address them? What must they do? Discuss.
7. Short and long term plans have different characteristics. Which items in the short-term plan that are not applicable in the long-term? What are the qualifications that incorporate with the short-term plan?
8. Why does a business plan start with an executive summary? What are the things planners want to emphasize? Discuss
9. Why do entrepreneurs need a good marketing analysis? Does good marketing analysis assure firms' potential return? If so, why and how? Discuss.
10. What are the benefits brought by R&D to the firm that despite its incurred amount it is still tolerable? How important is it in the business? Discuss.
11. In establishing a new venture, location is the top most consideration. What are its advantages to the firm? Discuss.
12. What are the important elements must management possess in contributing to business success?

KEY TERMS (in order of appearance)

business start-up	business plan	development plan
business ventures	benchmarking	SWOT analysis
strength	weaknesses	opportunities
threats	product dominance	strategic planning
short-tern plans	long-term plans	collated
problems	templates	marketing
analysis	research	development
proximity	management team	risk
forecasting	ROI	
oral presentation		

Works Cited

1. Africa Development Indicators, 2008/09. the Potential, the Problem, the Promise. Washington, D.C.: World Bank, 2009. Print.
2. Bashir, Asif, and Jeff Chan. Weaknesses. Birmingham: Unique Inspiration, 2015. Print.

3. Blitzer, Roy J. Hire Me, Inc.: Interviews. Irvine, CA: Entrepreneur, 2006. Print.
4. Butler, Carrie. Strength. Place of Publication Not Identified: Sapphire Star, 2013. Print.
5. Clements, Michael P., and David F. Hendry. The Oxford Handbook of Economic Forecasting. New York: Oxford UP, 2011. Print.
6. Cox, Jeff. The Venture: A Business Novel about Starting Your Own Company. New York, NY: Warner, 1997. Print.
7. Creating a Business Plan: Expert Solutions to Everyday Challenges. Boston, MA: Harvard Business School Pub., 2007. Print.
8. Creswell, John W. Research Design: Qualitative, Quantitative, and Mixed Method Approaches. Thousand Oaks, CA: Sage Publications, 2003. Print.
9. Doyle, Eleanor. The Economic System. Hoboken, NJ: John Wiley & Sons, 2005. Print.
10. Edison, Hali J. International Finance Discussion Papers: Asset Bubbles, Domino Effects and 'lifeboats' .. Place of Publication Not Identified: Bibliogov, 2013. Print.
11. Fine, Lawrence G. The SWOT Analysis: Using Your Strength to Overcome Weaknesses, Using Opportunities to Overcome Threats. Place of Publication Not Identified: Kick It, 2009. Print.
12. Gander, Ryan, and Stuart Bailey. Appendix. Amsterdam: Artimo, 2003. Print.
13. Gray, Amelia. Threats. New York: Farrar, Straus and Giroux, 2012. Print.
14. Harris, Michael. Opportunities. Harlow: Longman, 2003. Print.
15. Kearnes, Matthew, Matthew Kearnes, Francisco Reto. Klauser, and Stuart N. Lane. Critical Risk Research: Practices, Politics, and Ethics. Chichester, West Sussex: Wiley-Blackwell, 2012. Print.
16. Nelson, Rainbow. Panama: The Expansion Plan. London: Lloyd's List, 2005. Print.
17. Powell, Guy R., Steven Groves, and Jerry Dimos. ROI of $ocial Media: How to Improve the Return on Your Social Marketing Investment. Singapore: John Wiley & Sons (Asia), 2011. Print.
18. Schermerhorn, John R. Management. New York: J. Wiley, 2005. Print.
19. The Sevareid Issue. Bismarck, ND: North Dakota Humanities Council, 2010. Print.
20. Strategic Plan. Washington, DC: Office of the Federal Coordinator for Meteorological Services and Supporting Research, 2010. Print.
21. Takeyasu, Kazuhiro, Yasuo Ishii, and Yuki Higuchi. Marketing Analysis. Izumi: Izumi Syuppan, 2013. Print.
22. Tran, D. T. Process-oriented Semantic Web Search. Amsterdam: IOS, 2011. Print.
23. The Business Plan. Durant, OK: Oklahoma Small Business Development Center, 2005. Print.
24. S. Mariotti and C. Glackin, "Entrepreneurship", Starting and Operating a Small Business: Prentice Hall, 2010.

25. J.L Nelsen, "How to present your business plan" The Power of Unfair Advantage, www.Inc corporation, 2005

26. M. Porter, "Competitive Strategy". Techniques for Analyzing Industries and Competition", New York Press,1990.

27. Canfield, Bertrand R. "Sales Administration"-Principles and Problems, 4th edition, Prentice Hall.

28. Johnson H. Webster. "Sales Management Orientations, Administration 29. Marketing, Columbus, Ohio: Charles E. Merrill Publishing Company.

29. Walls, William T. Entrepreneurship Simplified- A Short Cut to Success, Chicago, New York: Opportunity Publishing Co., 2000.

INTERNET SITE ADDRESSES

For definition of strategic plan, see: *https://www.google.com.et/search* and *https://www.google.com.et/webhp*.

Chapter 4

THE PRODUCT CONCEPT

Introduction

Any product is not created accidentally. It comes from a strong idea generated and designed for consumers to meet their satisfaction. In layman's understanding, one may think that products are those tangible in nature; however, describing a product can be more than what an ordinary person defines it. In the concept of venturing marketing efforts, product is said to be a tangible materials that can be offered to the market for sale. This includes the total package such as the design, labelling, brand name, price, and other customer services such as warranty. One should not be misled between products against the services since products are tangible while services are not.

4. 1 WHAT IS A PRODUCT CONCEPT?

Some basic questions lead to product concept clarity. Why is there laundry soap? Why are there television sets? And why are there processed foods? Generally speaking, the enumerated items are not available in the early times. They are the products of the founder's strong imagination and creativity. The product concept details some sequential activity. The key activities include:

Idea generation stage

The first key activity of the process is the *idea generation*. This is the major task of the firm to conceptualize a product or services. The search for a good product is a continuous process that ensures product viability to the market. Several sources of product selection may derive from customers, competitors, distributors and dealers. However, sometimes ideas can be generated through nature. The concept of mineral drinking water did not derive from the above enumerated sources but was created through nature when typhoon Ruping devastated the Philippine area specifically in Cebu City where water became scarce and safety was not guarantee. Then, the mineral water was born. For an effective idea generation, the firm must answer the following questions:

Of what value are we delivering to customers?
What customer's problems are we trying to solve?
What specific type of products and services are we offering to each customer segment?
What customer's needs are we satisfying? Careful responses to the above questions will lead to a greater success for the firm in conducting a well-defined idea generation.

Idea screening

This activity secures the valuable information and disregards the pointless. Idea screening is very important considering that during the actual process, cost is inevitable; thus, proper investment must adhere to promising ideas. This stage seems critical to the investors since the next step involves monetary value so technical issues must be estimated well such as the target market, competition, price, market size, time element, production and expected return. There are underlying questions the firm must answer such as:

Is the product beneficial to both customers and society?
Is the product advertising valuable to the company?
Does it contribute to the realization of company's goals?
Does the business have the skilled people and resources to make the venture a success?
Does it increase company's patronage over the competitors?
Is there a clear access to distribution?
Is the advertising cost affordable?
Is the product technically workable?

Concept testing

It is a test that applies both quantitative and qualitative methods to assess the responsiveness of consumers to the product idea before its market introduction. In this stage, the firm considers three areas of the product as shown below.

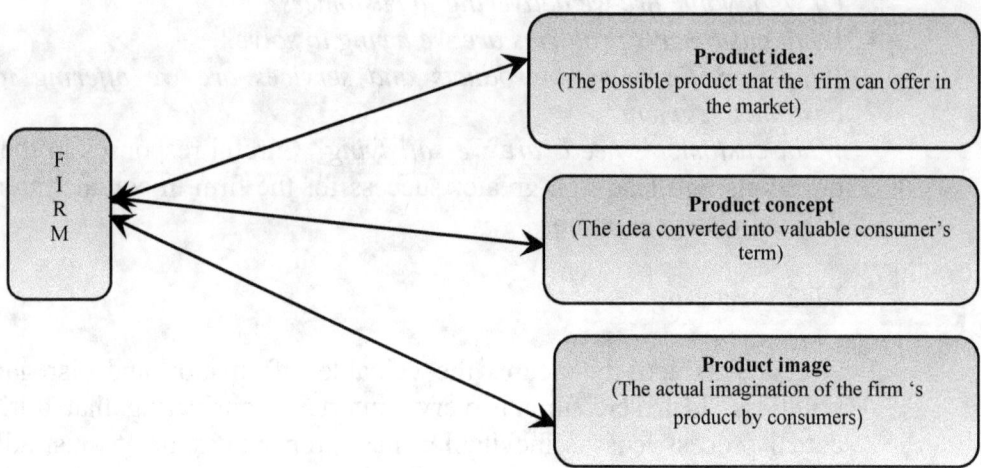

Figure 1 shows the firm's perspective during the concept testing stage.

The above illustration brings a big challenge to the firm considering that every new product introduced in the market expects to have different views from consumers down to competitors. For the firm to be prepared with these possibilities, they must confidently answer some critical questions as enumerated below.

What competitive value does the new concept have in terms of quality and reliability over the competitors?

Is our concept strong enough to compete the existing products in the market place?

Is the market opportunity sustainable for future possible business expansion?

How are the products integrated in the customer's routine?

This activity is technically testing the new product concept or sometimes called test market where the activity is focused on the target group of consumers purposely to get some feedbacks regarding the product. Feedbacks are potential information for the firm to benchmark some product improvement or modification if necessary for a better production.

Product development stage

Product development stage requires a good foundation such as the creation of new product with unique characteristics that bring new or substantial benefits to target customers. It also involves some modifications for an existing product or it exhibits a new product that can satisfy the newly created group of customers or marketers. It is a test of a product to ensure convincing results prior to its elevation to the next level by the product development concern. It is usually the firm's research and development (R&D) that is responsible to make an architectural design to conceptualize the physical product. However, they must ensure that the required functional features are present and must convey the desired psychological uniqueness. The product development stage suggests having some qualifying questions for the firm to ensure its realization, some of these are:

What skills and resources are needed and how are they acquired?
Are the resources expensive?
Where can the skills and resources be sought?

Test marketing stage

This is experimental on the part of the firm. This step is designed by the firm to ensure that making a decision to pursue the venture gives them the assurance of meeting their main objectives considering that mass production would entail an enormous amount of financial resources. It also incorporates in the testing process the product positioning strategy, advertising, methods of distribution and the like to ascertain that test marketing will provide knowledge on how dealers and consumers react to the new product. As guiding notes, this activity necessitates that firm to consider the following questions:

Through which channels does the customer segment want to be reached?
How can the firm reach them?
How efficient are the firm's distribution channels?

Commercialization

The last step in the process is the launching of the product where the physical product is already available for commercializing. The firm should make a careful decision and analysis on how to make the activity most efficient since this entails an extra ordinary cost. There are many ways to launch a product depending on the capacity of the firm. Large firms can make it a more dazzling one by using different media outlet that can help them create a wider scope of coverage; however, the bigger the expenditures spent for launching more efforts are needed for recovering such cost and on the process, it will demand for high volume of sales. Some firms effectively strategize the product launching economically.

They introduce the products directly to the consumers and gain immediate feedbacks from them. In the real sense, doing the commercialized activity, firms usually have in mind the questions as to when, where, whom, and how the product is. However, answering the underlying questions can be better done by considering the different elements needed. Below suggest some tips for a successful commercialization process:

As to when the launching can be done, firm should consider it like if some big events are coming; proper scheduling must be set for the identified occasions. People are the key factor for a successful launching activity; hence, identifying some important events to come is very ideal. The recent visit of Pope Francis in the Philippines united millions of Filipino people from different sectors and was a great opportunity for businesses to sell their products and gained a lot.

Answering the question of where, requires the firm to reasonably identify the scope where the product will be launched. It can be on selected areas like regional, provincial or national depending on the identified scope by the firm.

To answer the question of to whom, it is necessary that the firm will be able to identify the target groups with their profiles so the firm can determine their buying capacity to make their business profitable.

Answering the question of how is somewhat technical. It requires an appropriate action plan to clearly identify the different approaches and strategies to be used. To successfully address the question, it is important to select which target market to be selected first.

4.2 PHASES OF A PRODUCT

After its conceptualization, the real product comes tangible; however, it is very important to know its nature and its elements.

Product defined

A typical person buys something to satisfy his wants which can be a product or a service. If one pays for a haircut it is a service but if he needs a cone of ice-cream it is exactly a good. The classification of products and services will be discussed in the succeeding part of this chapter. For a clearer understanding, here are some definitions of a product.

What is product?

Products are tangible items that bear figurative features purposely created to satisfy a consumer's wants and needs. Sample products are like car, television set, computers, laptop, cellular phones, etc. which answer varying human needs. All kinds of products are made of three components called as phases such as:

- The core product
- The actual product
- Augmented product

The core product

This part of the product mainly focuses on providing the solution to customer's need. It consists of the benefits any buyer aims at buying. For example, one buys a soft drink to quench his thirst.

The actual product

This is an output based on the core product that carries the total package like content, product name/brand name, quality, design and other features. In general, actual products are those ready for disposal to customers. For example, the core product of a soft drink is the substance itself; however, it has to undergo a process of putting the substance inside the bottle to make it an actual product. After which, it must be sealed and labelled with all vital information attached to make the actual product complete. It must bear a unique image in order to capture the customer's interest.

The augmented product

These are additional benefits inherent from the core and the actual product created to delight customers by giving them more than what they expect out of buying. Nowadays competition is vastly increasing; Firm should initiate some exciting moves keeping their customers. Augmentation is an initiative of providing customers value added services so that firms do not only compete in terms of quality, price, and other types of in-store competition but in the aspect of augmentation as well. Buying a product today does not end when payment and delivery are done. It must incorporate in the products some friendly user's information which serves as their guide. The warranty certificate which includes the repair and maintenance is a part of product augmentation.

4.3 PRODUCT PROTECTION

Product as an intellectual property needs to be protected to ensure that the ownership of the invention will be preserved by the founder. There are ways to protect the product, namely: patent, trademark and copyright.

Technical differences between patent, trademark and copyright

Patent

This is a privilege granted to the founder or an inventor who develops the product or even the process to ensure that the particular activity is protected. This is issued by the government giving the owner the authority to make, use and sell its products for a number of years freely. A patent incorporates specific statement that describes the founder's invention which specifies therein the exact details to be protected by patent.

Trademark

It is a total product description distinct from the competitors. The term trademark includes word, name, tag lines, letters or number, symbol, design and color combination. The trademarks bring to people the ease of recognition of the product sources by just looking the elements of the trade mark. The familiar tag line that reminds the people in availing the bank services like *"We find ways"* is immediately linked to BDO. LBC's popular slogan, *"We deliver like no tomorrow"*. PRULIFE U.K assures, *"Always Listening, Always Understanding"*. Easy recognition is one of the many benefits of trademark that increases awareness and later creates customer's loyalty. In general, trademark builds customer's trust.

Copyrights

This is a protection given to people who engage in written works. The span of time for copyrights is based on the extent of life plus 50 years. This activity protects the symbol, the year and the author's name. It gives authority to the concerned to have the exclusive right to produce, reproduce and distribute outputs to the public for its use. Anyone can be charged for plagiarism if caught copying the work and commercializing it.

4.5 PRODUCT CLASSIFICATIONS

As defined earlier, product refers to tangible items created to satisfy consumer's needs and wants. Each product entails different impact to life of the users; hence, products need to be classified according to their varying use. If the product is good for direct consumption, it is said to be consumer's product. On the other hand, if the product is used as source for further creation of another form, it is an industrial product. Below enumerate the different classes of products:

Suitable products
Spending products
Field products
Unsolicited products

Suitable products

These are the products frequently purchased with a minimal effort. Daily consumptions like milk, rice, spices, toiletries and the like are available 24/7 and very accessible to any store nearby. This has been mushrooming around to cater the buying behaviour of customers.

Spending products

Products like these create a sudden demand if buyers find some advantages to them. The increasing level of competition today and the growing number of sellers trigger businessmen to create some attractions to buyers. Price reduction is one common practice today that entices buyers to buy more by offering reduced price. Consumers only respond and spend their money if they find it advantageous to them and quickly do shopping. The SM malls nationwide practice this kind of activity regularly and finds it very effective. They are able to capture the market and sustain their operation using this approach. The price reduction applies mostly to furniture, clothing, shoes, bags and etc.

Field products

Buying these products is usually a luxury by nature. Its price is high because it carries a status symbol with selective buyers. In the Philippines, the most dominant car brand is Toyota on top of other brands. Lexus and Safari are seldom seen like vintage cars. Contrary in Qatar where there are only two kinds of people, the rich and the very rich, Toyota brand is less popular compared to high class, Lexus, Safari and Lamborghini. In general, the field product is not designed to ordinary people due to its price brought about by quality and uniqueness.

Unsolicited products

These products do not have the recognition of their need. The introduction of insurance business at the start does not have enough share for budget allocation to prospect buyer until such a time that the need recognition arises. This holds true to funeral business that in the early stage people don't dare from buying until such time they realize the value.

4.6 THE PRODUCT LIFE AND ITS CYCLE

Any form of product including human life is not exempted to experience the so-called life cycle. In the case of business, product life cycle is very crucial considering that it will endanger investment and business will face risk in the operation.

What is a product life cycle?

It is the evolution of a product starting from its introduction (birth), growth, stability and decline. The firm cannot escape from this reality so proper understanding on how to handle the situation is a must. Below illustrates the structure of product life cycle.

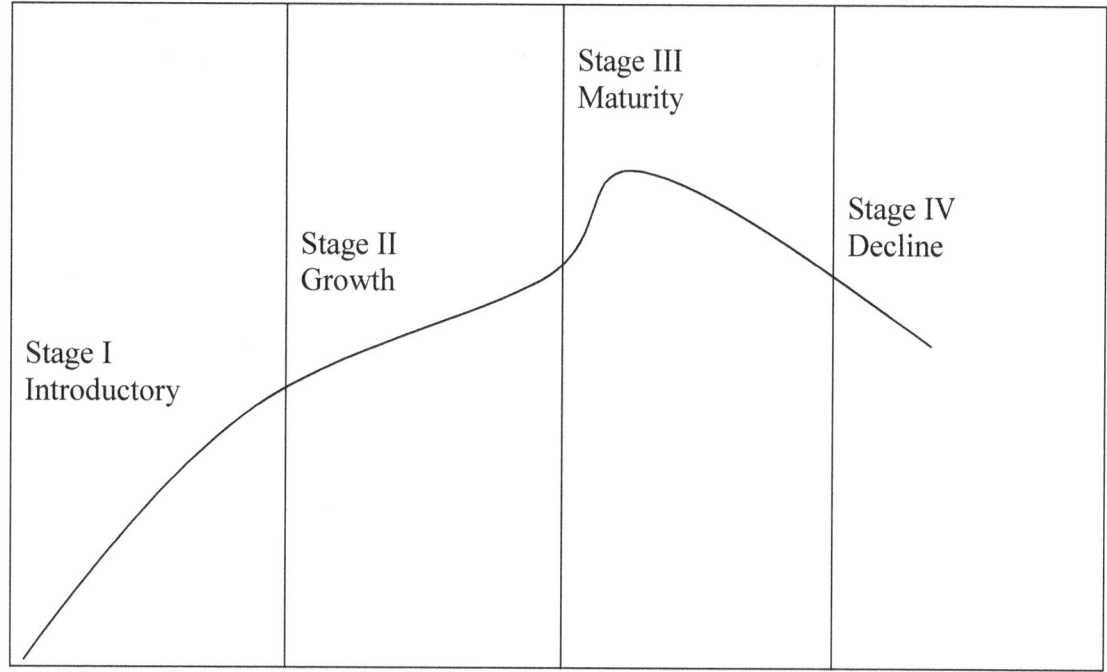

Figure 2 shows the model of product life cycle

Introductory stage

The first stage of the product cycle is when the firm exhausts all possible efforts and resources in order that the product can penetrate in the market to capture sales and attention of buyers. This activity requires the firm to employ some strategies such as face to face selling not only to sales outlets but to end users as well. In this stage, it is imperative for the firm to be creative by using some promotional activities to attract buyers considering that the product is not yet known to the target market. More focus is needed at this stage. For the business to succeed in this endeavour, the firm should address first the following questions:

Which activity in this stage is given priority?
What distribution channel must be used?
How can customer and users' relationship be developed?
What values are delivered to the customers?
What strategies must be employed to help the customers solve their problems?
What specific products are offered to the target segments?

How can customers be satisfied? Prompt answers to the above questions will lead the business to success in the first stage of the cycle. Most importantly, the firm must ensure that the customers have meaningful experiences to remember about their products.

Growth

The growth stage usually depends on how effective are the introductory efforts. During the growth stage, however, mostly there is an occurrence of abnormal movement (fast moving) brought about by the self-advertising or word of mouth of the customers who entice others to buy. This is very critical for the firm; therefore, they should take advantage of the momentum and consider that at this level, firm must realize a portion of profit from investment. Some products may show growth in the early stage but may not sustain. Here are some tips to keep the product growing.

Get customers and dealers' feedback
What strategy must be employed to keep the momentum going?
What terms can be offered to dealers to make them loyal to the firm?
What do salesmen need to maintain?
How can customers and dealers be protected from competition?
How can customers be delighted continuously?

Maturity

At this level, a product becomes stable and continues to generate profit for the firm. However, firm should take a closer look at this point and make no mistake or be over confident considering that competitors are just waiting for the opportunity to capture the market. Heavy advertising is needed to keep a larger market share. It is a fact that if a product's sale reaches the peak level its sales performance starts to experience maturity which requires the firm to initiate some moves to keep the product on top. The prolonged maturity is also crucial to the firm because no one controls the time; hence, vigilance on the part of the firm is needed. To protect the product momentum in the maturity stage, firms should ask themselves the following questions:

What strategic preparations do we have?
What are the competitors doing?
How responsive our customers are?
What promotional reinforcement do we need?
What initiative do we need to make our product a good choice?

Decline

This stage of product life cycle conveys a message that the product may experience obsolescence. Any product can become obsolete when a modern one comes into the market which requires the firm to make innovation or modification in order to regain market leadership. A typical telephone system becomes obsolete due to the introduction of cellular phones. A key pad model fades due to the introduction of touch screen type. A big typical television set also becomes obsolete due to the introduction of the flat screen models. Since nothing is permanent in business, it is suggested that in order for the firm to stay in the market, the keys are modification and innovation.

4.7 WAYS TO EXTEND PRODUCT LIFE

No firm can ever prevent a product from declining notwithstanding, the efforts exerted upon. It is indeed a business' nature. However, there are several ways of extending the life span of every product such as Extending beyond market limit, Educating users for other product use, Inviting more users, and increasing area coverage.

Extending beyond market limit

Every firm understands its individual limitation despite its capacity. One of the many ways is searching for a new market. The major factor why life of a certain product declines is due to the presence of many identical products and close substitutes. Competing them results to an increase of operating expenditures for the firm. Instead of competing them head-to-head, the best strategy is to expand firm's market. The bottom line in business competition is "penetration"; however, total penetration is very impossible for the firm to do. As the demand for the product grows, the firm tends to concentrate on sales volume and neglect other buyer's attention. Extending new markets, below suggest the following tips for the firm to do:

What distribution channel will be used and how to do it?
What market segment will be concentrated?
What marketing strategy is applicable?
What promotional strategy will bring impact to the new market?

These guide questions are beneficial for the firm to succeed in their venture. Firm should be aware of the principle, *"Success is equal to preparedness plus opportunity"*.

Educating users for other product use

A product is designed for consumption and satisfying specific needs. Users may buy a product for a purpose of satisfying their mindset like buying milk. If its benefit is only for drinking, there is a big tendency for the product to decline considering the competition around it. Educating buyers for the other use of the product will create another new market. For example, if the buyer discovers that milk has more uses over and above the main purpose of drinking they will capitalize this for their advantage. Products known to have very strong competition must extend their product life. To do so, the firm must be aware and be able to answer the questions below:

What are the skills needed to do it?
Which key activities must be performed?
What impact does the activity give to the revenue?
What values are delivered to the customers?
How can customers be enticed?
Every endeavour needs a careful analysis and planning so if the firm can address the above questions; these merit their success in educating the users for other product use.

Inviting more users

This strategy is designed to invite more users for the product to sustain life cycle. This activity would mean searching customers who have not yet used the product. After identifying them through a research or a survey, firm should initiate a move of inviting them to use the product.

Increasing area of coverage

The firm usually identifies area to cover for their products simply because of the cost consideration. Expanding into a larger market would create a domino effect in terms of financial requirements, manpower and other resources needed. To sustain and remain in the industry, the firm should decide a gradual span of coverage such as regional, national and even international in scope.

4.8 THE ROLE OF PRICE TO A PRODUCT

Price is always the determinant of the product sold in the market. Without the price attached to the product, it will not give meaning to the industry; hence, price and product are inseparable. Pricing a certain commodity is always based on the total cost of producing every unit of it. Due to strong competition, firms design an activity on how to attract buyers and to sustain in business as well. In designing a pricing strategy, firm should consider the following questions:

What is the present demand status?
How responsive are customers to lower price?
How many product substitutes are available in the market?
How is price reduction done?
How to measure firms benefit?

What is demand?

It is generally referred to the desire for goods and services. This desire will remain as it is in the absence of the ability and willingness to buy. What hinders buyers for not fulfilling the said demand is their capacity of buying. Demand is the yardstick for every firm since a product is nothing if they fail to determine the demand. Demand by nature has a boundless relationship to price considering that in the real world, as price increases, demand starts to decrease. In Economics, it is "ceteris paribus" which means other things remain constant. For a clearer understanding, below illustrate the relationships between demand and price.

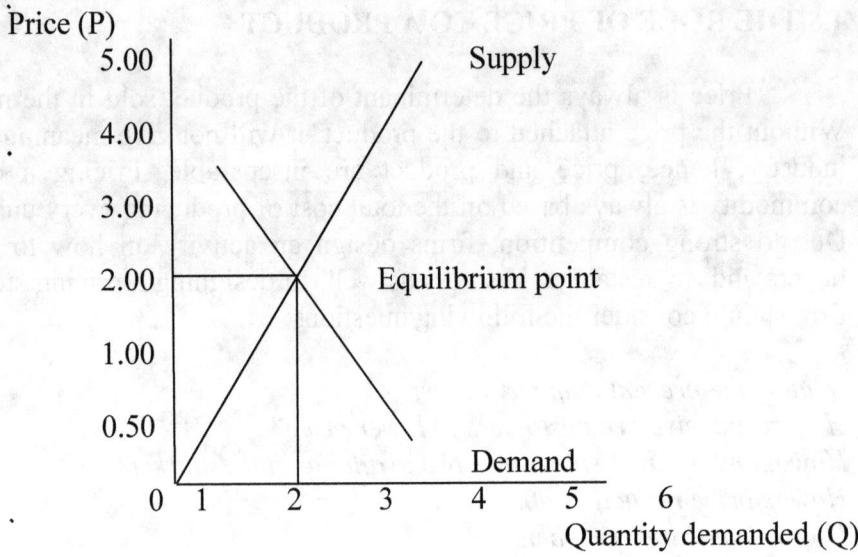

Figure 3 shows the relationships between price and demand

The above illustration shows that the quantity demanded by buyers is 5 at P 2.00 which means that the buyer's willingness to buy is up to the price of P 2.00. If the commodity's price increases, it correspondingly affects the demand. The diagram below illustrates how demand is affected by change in price.

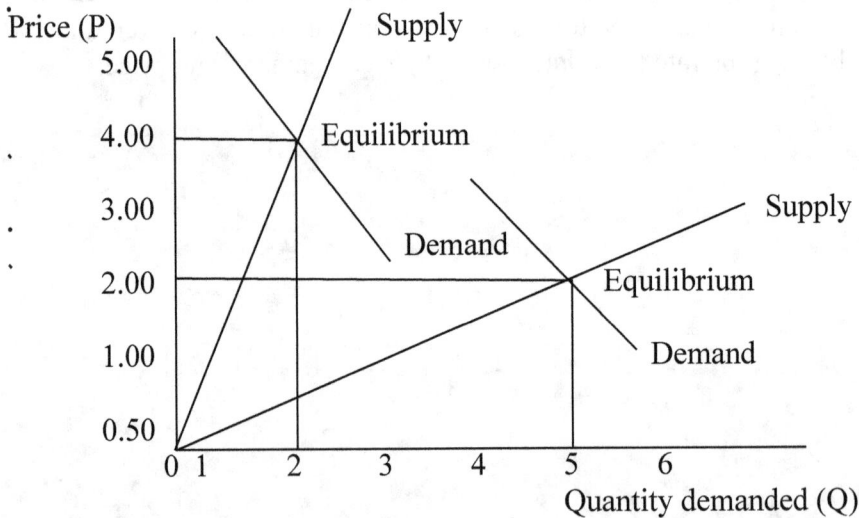

Figure 4 shows the effect of demand brought about by increase in price.

The above illustration shows the impact of demand when the price of commodity increases. The price increase for the firm is necessary in order to cover the cost of production and other governmental requirements such as taxes and licenses; hence, price changes oftentimes happen. The impact of price change to demand creates a new equilibrium. Although the firm is trying to keep the price of their commodity affordable to consumers, it is impossible due to the presence of competition and other requirements.

Factors that create price change

- Presence of substitute products
- Government requirements
- Advertising expenses
- Complementary goods
- Population

Factors that contribute demand change

- Change in product preferences
- Entry of new competing products
- Income
- Obsolescence

Firms should be aware of the above factors considering that they will bring forth some unfavorable impact to their business.

The essence of price off to buyer's responsiveness

Most companies strategize some moves in order to keep their customers; however, it is necessary to properly determine its impact to revenue generating by the firm. One of the measures is to use is the application of elasticity so the firm can benchmark the effect of the strategy used. Price reduction needs a careful analysis since both profit generation and customers are of the same value for the firm. Profits are generated through sales and sales are contributed by buyers; hence, they bring the same element that firm should consider. Lowering price change attracts buyers but reduces firm's revenue. While higher price change increases firm's revenue but reduces the number of buyers. These scenarios require strategic analysis to facilitate smooth operation. For a clearer view, consider some illustrations below.

Sample Problem

The Marie Antigua Corporation, a famous maker of ladies' wears experiences sales reduction which affects its revenue due to price increase. The manager opts a price off activity hoping to generate more sales. He needs to know at what level, price reduction increases sales and at what point, price increase reduces revenue. Information is shown below.

Price	Item sold
30	20
25	15
20	10
10	5

The formula of elasticity is used to determine the result that will guide the manager in his decision making on the proposed plan.

Formula

$$\partial p = \frac{I_2 - I_1}{P_2 - P_1} \times \frac{P_2 + P_1}{I_2 + I_1}$$

Where:
∂P = Change in price (increase/decrease)
I_1 = item sold at price 1
I_2 = item sold at price 2
P_1 = price for item 1
P_2 = price for item 2

Given:
P_1 = 30
P_2 = 25
I_1 = 20
I_2 = 15

Solution:

$$\frac{20-15}{} \times \frac{25+30}{} = 5 \times 55 \quad\quad 275$$

$$\frac{25-30}{20+15} = -5 \times 35 \quad -175$$

= 275/-175

= 1.57

The above illustration shows that when the manager deducts the price of P 5.00 from P 30.00 which becomes 25.00, approximately the number of buyers will increase by 1.57 percent. On the contrary, before the manager makes a decision, he needs to know also of what percent does the price increase affect the sales. Information is shown below.

Price	Items sold
30	20
35	25
40	30
45	35

Formula:
$$\circ p = \frac{I2 - I1}{P2 - P1} \times \frac{P2 + P1}{I2 + I1}$$

Given:
P1 = 30
P2 = 35
I1 = 20
I2 = 25

Solution:

$$\frac{25-20}{35-30} \times \frac{35+30}{25+20} = \frac{5 \times 65}{-5 \times 45} \quad \frac{325}{-225}$$

= 325/-225

= 1.44

After the inquiries conducted, the manager has to make a crucial decision whether he pursues his price-off plan or not. It reveals that the two activities don't have significant effect to the business considering that the buyers are unresponsive. Hence, making a realistic decision matters a lot.

4.9 OTHER WAYS TO AID REVENUE GENERATION FOR THE FIRM

Business by nature is money making device. It requires the financial managers to find other alternatives or business avenues to generate other forms of income to aid and sustain varying operational needs. Most successful finance managers are good in spotting opportunity where they can put their surplus funds in sourcing out other forms of revenue. Using a portion of retained earnings of the firm will help strengthen their financial standing. Wise choice of investment is guided with the principles of the time value of money.

What is time value of money?

By definition, it is the value of money generated through an investment and time is the basic element for the money to grow. The longer the time of investment the better is the return. Buying stocks is one of the best avenues to put an investment but it is risky. Buying an insurance is also considered as best investment alternative for it promises a good future financial return. However, a good investment can be judged depending on the amount generated from it. A good financial manager must ascertain the return of investment which can be measured through interest rates. One common approach is the use of the time value of money. To appreciate this approach, consider some illustrative samples shown below.

Sample problem:

Suppose you have $ 50,000 at hand and you invested this amount at 12 percent compounded annually for a period of 5, 8, and 10 years how much will your money be at the end of the given period? We will compute it using the numbers of years since it was invested to determine the importance of time in an investment.

Solution:

For 5 years investment period, your money grows to

$ 50,000 (1.12)5 = $ 88,117.08

For 8 years investment period, your money grows to

$ 50,000 (1.12)8   = 123,798.16

For 10 years of investment period, your money grows to

$ 50,000 (1.12)10   = 155,292.41

It can be gleaned from above that investment grows even if the interest rate is constant but the time element is longer. Therefore, time is the essence of every investment.

Doubling your money

Another illustration can help the investors to determine if their investment doubles its value. This approach is critical to those who have no concrete knowledge about computing when they invest on time to double the value of their money. Some business scams offer an investment to prospects and promise to double their money in shorter period such a three months. This is impossible considering that the determinant of doubling your money is the interest rate. For a wider understanding of this principle, two formulas are commonly used such as Rule 72 and Rule 69 with a constant factor of 0.35. Rule 72 was formerly used by businessmen but later changed to Rule 69 using the constant factor.

Sample problem:

John has $ 50,000 on his account and when he invests it, he wants to know when can his money be doubled? It must be noted that the determinant factor is the interest rate. If John invests that amount in two different interest rates, how do the varying rates affect his investment?

Using the formula of Rule 69 plus constant factor of 0.35

Interest rates   projected years in doubling

12 percent	0.35 + 69/12	= 6.1 years
13 percent	0.35 + 69/13	= 5.6 years
15 percent	0.35 + 69/15	= 4.96 years

The results imply that if the interest rate is lower, the time element to make it double is high. Hence, John should choose to invest his money at the rate of 15 percent giving him only 4.96 or 5 years waiting time for his money to double its value.

SUMMARY

Creation of a product is designed for customer's consumption and does not come into actual and tangible accidentally. Proper understanding on the process is needed on the part of its founder in order to achieve its desired purpose.

The conceptualization of a product can be realized by soliciting ideas or from the experiences of the maker. The existing product in the market today comes from the exerted effort of the firm so that the information gathered will lead to a potential creation of a new product or innovation to suit the need of the end users.

In the development of the product there are series of activities to be done starting from the first stage of idea generation up to commercializing. This activity demands for a technical process considering that it is sensitive to its actual product realization. Successful product realization should be guided by some technical questions leading to produce appropriate final output.

The concept testing on the other hand applies the quantitative and qualitative methods as a means of assessing buyer's responsiveness. In the course of the process, firm projects three elements that include product idea, product concept, and product image.

Test marketing stage is experimental on the part of the firm. This is done to ensure that the main objectives are successfully attained Producing a certain product demands for an enormous amount of financial resources; thus, strategies, methods and other components must be clearly defined.

The final aim of production is commercializing. The activity should be done in an orderly manner in order to promote an awareness to buyers so the resources and marketing activities will surely result to a favourable impact to the firm.

Production involves different phases that require the management to define carefully the activities around it. A product consists of three elements namely; the core, final and augmented. Taking care of a product does not end if it is already sold. After sales service, augmentation is needed especially that competition is continuous in this process as it conveys customer care. Producing a product is not easy since effort, financial and other resources are involved; hence, it is safe to give protection to them such as providing the patent, trademarks and copyright to protect founder's ownerships.

Product has different classifications designed to fit customer's use. Different product creations would mean different users enjoying them. Product classification varies up to the extent that it defines the users.

Every product has its own life cycle. Its extent depends largely on the owner as he finds ways to secure it.

In the market, a product is always attached with a price and its absence is meaningless. Both are inseparable to determine the worth of anything sold for a price. Price as an important element serves as tool for marketers to determine how buyers respond to a product. Nowadays, competition is very strong and becoming stronger; hence, some strategies can be employed such as price reduction but careful analysis prior to implementation must be done.

The management must always find possible means of investment in order to generate other forms of revenue to aid operational cost. The finance manager must be equipped with technical skills and strategies to initiate and design some investment vehicles to augment revenue other than what the business is really doing. They also need to know the principles of the time value of money as they continue to strive for business success.

DISCUSSION QUESTIONS

1. Why do founders strive to produce a product despite knowing the constraints and other difficulties of doing it? Discuss.
2. Discuss the product concept and enumerate some major impacts to the firm if it fails?
3. What are the potential contributions of idea screening and why does the firm need it? Discuss.
4. If the final product caries the important elements attached to it, what is a core product? And what are the reasons of the customers for buying it? Discuss.
5. Patent, trademarks and copyrights are product protections. In what way they can give protection and up to what extent is the protection span? Discuss.

6. What is the purpose of product classifications and why does the firm need to do it? Explain.
7. In the captured market share, explain the statement, "product after reaching maturity needs to be replaced?
8. Name at least one activity that extends product life and discuss how must the firm do it?
9. Why is price very essential to the product and why are they inseparable? Explain
10. Discuss the relationship between demand and price. How do these elements affect the firm in realizing its goals?
11. Discuss the essence of time value of money in the business and its contribution to revenue generation?

KEY TERMS (in order of their appearance)

product concept	idea screening	market size	Venture
feedbacks	modifications	substantial benefits	
enormous	commercialization	conceptualization	core
product	augmentation intellectual property		suitable
products	unsolicited products	field products	spending
products	product life cycle	pricing strategy	
boundless	relationships	ceteris paribus	buyer's
responsiveness	time value of money		

Works Cited

1. Belz, Andrea. Product Development. Maidenhead: McGraw-Hill Professional, 2011. Print.
2. Boothroyd, G., Peter Dewhurst, and W. A. Knight. Product Design for Manufacture and Assembly. Boca Raton, Fl: CRC, 2011. Print.
3. Cavusgil, S. Tamer., Gary A. Knight, and John R. Riesenberger. International Business: The New Realities. Upper Saddle River, NJ: Prentice Hall/Pearson, 2012. Print.
4. Cohen, William A. The Marketing Plan. Hoboken, NJ: J. Wiley & Sons, 2006. Print.
5. Credland, P. F. Advances in Stored Product Protection: Proceedings of the 8th International Working Conference on Stored Product Protection, 22-26 July 2002, York, UK. Cambridge, MA: CAB International, 2003. Print.
6. Dalrymple, Douglas J., and Leonard J. Parsons. Basic Marketing Management. New York: Wiley, 2000. Print.

7. Dalrymple, Douglas J., and Leonard J. Parsons. Basic Marketing Management. New York: Wiley, 2000. Print.
8. Elias, Stephen, and Richard Stim. Trademark: Legal Care for Your Business & Product Name. Berkeley, CA: Nolo, 2010. Print.
9. Field, Marilyn J., and Thomas F. Boat. Rare Diseases and Orphan Products: Accelerating Research and Development. Washington, D.C.: National Academies, 2010. Print.
10. Foster, Harold M. Crossing Over: Teaching Meaning-centered Secondary English Language Arts. Mahwah, NJ: L. Erlbaum Associates, 2002. Print.
11. Gabka, Christian J., Heinz Bohmert, and Phillip N. Blondeel. Plastic and Reconstructive Surgery of the Breast. Stuttgart: Thieme, 2009. Print.
12. Gorges, Arthur. His Majesties Letters Pattent for an Office Called the Publicke Register for Generall Commerce. Amsterdam: Theatrum Orbis Terrarum, 1974. Print.
13. Illustration-based Health Information Messages: Concept Testing. Ottawa: Public Opinion Research & Evaluation Division, Health Canada, 2006. Print.
14. Kotler, Philip, and Gary Armstrong. Principles of Marketing. Boston: Pearson Prentice Hall, 2012. Print.
15. Kotler, Philip, and Gary Armstrong. Principles of Marketing. Boston: Pearson Prentice Hall, 2012. Print.
16. Kotler, Philip, and Philip Kotler. A Framework for Marketing Management. Upper Saddle River, NJ: Prentice Hall, 2001. Print.
17. Krasilovsky, M. William., Sidney Shemel, John M. Gross, and Jonathan Feinstein. This Business of Music. New York: Billboard, 2007. Print.
18. Lindert, Peter H. Growing Public: Social Spending and Economic Growth since the Eighteenth Century. Cambridge, UK: Cambridge, 2004. Print.
19. Oxlade, Chris. Growth. Chicago, IL: Raintree, 2012. Print.
20. Perry, Yaron. British Mission to the Jews in Nineteenth-century Palestine. London: Frank Cass, 2003. Print.
21. Ravenhill, Mark, and Mark Ravenhill. Product. London: Bloomsbury, 2013. Print.
22. Slywotzky, Adrian J., and Karl Weber. Demand: Creating What People Love before They Know They Want It. New York: Crown Business, 2011. Print.
23. Things Are Not as They Seem. Palmerston, N.T.: Palmerston Own Writers, 2014. Print.

24. Time Value of Money: Keystrokes, CFA. Middletown, OH: Keir Educational Resources, 2003. Print.
25. Verhage, Bronislaw, Ph Waalewijn, and A. J. Van Weele. New Product Development in Dutch Companies: The Idea Generation Stage. Delft: Interuniversitaire Interfaculteit Bedrijfskunde, 1982. Print.
26. Vitale, Robert P., Joseph J. Giglierano, and Waldemar Pfoertsch. Business-to-business Marketing: Analysis and Practice. Boston: Prentice Hall, 2011. Print.
27. Yoo, Christopher S. Copyright. Cheltenham, UK: Edward Elgar Pub., 2011. Print
28. D. A. Aaker, "Brand Relevance: Making Competitor Relevant",
29. Hoboken, Nj: Jossey-Bass Publisher, 2011.
30. M. Porter, "Competitive Strategy; Techniques for Analyzing Industries and Competitors: New York: Free Press, 1980.
31. G. George and A.J Bock, "The Business Models and Its Implications for Entrepreneurs Research, Entrepreneurship Theory and Practice, 2011.
32. R.A. Baron and J. Tang, "The Role of Entrepreneurship in the Firm-Level Innovation, Journal for Business Venturing, 2002.
33. M. Porter, Competitive Advantage: Creating and Sustaining 34. Superior Performance, New York Free Press, 1995.

INTERNET SITE ADDRESSES

1. https://www.google.com.et/webhp
2. http://www.businessdictionary.com/definition/product-development.html

Chapter 5

MANAGING ENTREPRENEURIAL GROWTH

Introduction

Since the preliminary part, each chapter of this book presents the rudiments of doing business and the various challenges a firm confronts with its start-ups. Many people can make things possible to happen due to their skills and perseverance yet the management plays a vital role. There are a lot of entrants who try their luck in business, become successful at a start but gradually deteriorate because they find difficulty in managing the business. Some firms tend to be very active in marketing their products until everything becomes stable but in the later part of the game, it is the competitor who leads in the market. The common problem is the ability to overcome obstacles resulting to product declines. Business particularly in marketing needs people who are strong-willed and perseverant to work on business with "no mercy" principles. They will take all measures to get an edge or surpass the competitors for the good of the firm.

5.1 IMPORTANCE OF MARKET POSITIONING

The secret of being a successful businessman or woman in the world of business is finding their right position. Prior to Seven Eleven (7/11) company's expansion, a careful study was being made. They want to ensure that once the business is established, it will create an impact to buyers and stakeholders. They aim to target youngsters and adults particularly. As observed, they are mushrooming in nearby schools where students are their primary customers. This also holds true to Jollibee, a world renowned food chain which has succeeded in the food business through the use of strategic positioning. Positioning is a process of identifying who are your target markets. When Jollibee was introduced in the Philippines it projected a marketing strategy that identifies their target markets with no less than the children including their parents. Their adds strongly invite children to dine and play with them. Parents who love and support their children will come with them to enjoy their bonding. The depicted family culture is a strong capture for Filipino food lovers. The information and experiences cited above give enthusiasts some business ideas on how to segment the business activity clearly. Segmenting the product lines needs expertise who can use the business models as guiding

principles. As stated by *U.C Berkely* some key activities are beneficial to a business He enlists as well several questions for the firm to address?
1. What key activities are required in the market positioning?
2. What is the importance of market positioning?
3. What customer's conditions must be satisfied?
4. How important are these to the customers?

The segmentation process

Firms offer various products to different levels of customers purposely to compete and determine the market potentials. This is done by the firm to ensure effectiveness of the marketing activity, address customer's desire and above all, maximize the limited resources of the firm. This process is called segmentation .It classifies customers with their product use. It also helps facilitates and guide them on how to go about and provide them a clear direction in making the process effective. The process calls for **geographical** locations:
- Province
- City
- Region
- Nation

The above enumerated items give the firms an idea in terms of setting priorities as to where to focus their resources and draw a plan of activity strategically. As it is said resources are limited; hence, using them effectively through a well-defined segmentation process will help the firms realize their set objectives.

Another factor affecting the segmentation process is the demographics. Customer's personal background can be a gauge in producing a product for a target market. The d**emographics** consist of:
- Age
- Gender
- Family size
- Income

The third element in the segmentation process is **psychographics**. These include personality, lifestyle and values. The customer's character, choice of activities and norms play a potent factor in his or her preferences. His choices are labelled according to what he believes is right and what makes him happy and satisfied. Personal expenditures are always affected by psychographics. Thus, it is imperative for the firm to know these factors for an expected favourable return.

Some guiding questions are given to make an effective segmentation:
1. Which key activities does our valuable proposition require?
2. What values do we deliver to the customer?
3. Which customer's problem does the company try to solve?
4. What bundles of products and services are offered to each customer segment?
5. What is the most important cost which is inherent to the task?

The segmentation model

The segmentation model shows the process in terms of selecting specific market and the strategic positioning. The activity involves grouping and identifying product of similar preference, identifying the target group and strategy to be used. Figure 1 shows the segmentation process.

Step 1	Step 2	Step 3
Activity →	Activity	Activity
Identifying what group in the market and product of similar preferences.	Which of these groups are we targeting and how to do it?	What strategy to use in order to attract potential customers?

Table 1 shows the steps in segmentation process

5.2 THE TARGET MARKET

Underlying various types of market, it is imperative for the firm and the new entrants to identify which market to serve in order to effectively use limited resources as discussed earlier. Serving different types of market could be difficult for the firm to focus their skills and resources; hence, it is suggested to identify which one to concentrate first. Market targeting requires some guidelines to succeed in the endeavour. Below enumerate some key activities:

Key activities
1. Which market must be prioritized?
2. How potential is the market?
3. Which key activities are identified?
4. What key resources are needed?

5. How much will it cost to do?
6. How much revenue does each stream contribute?

Based on the above, the firm can now identify which potential target market to cater first depending on the firm's capacity. However, it is vital to start serving the target market that has potential. What matters to the firm is the overall return and it is suggested to start on a market niche. This is described as the group of people in the society that possess the same common interest.

Positioning Requirements

The selection of the target market is done; the next challenge of the firm is establishing the right position with an aim to be different from its competitors. Good positioning can be an advantage to the firm in executing their strength. In the world of competition, *"may the best firm win"* and winning is an output of good positioning. Business positioning can lead to business success. There are different approaches in product positioning. A product display in the mall requires the merchandiser to position his products in a strategic manner that it can catch the attention of the prospect buyers like a product seen directly on the eye level. Positioning also in the case of establishing a warehouse requires strategic location with an easy access to major selling activity. Location can be more understood using the following criteria.

A good and strong position defined as:
- ✓ Accessible
- ✓ Reachable
- ✓ Comfortable

Accessible as an element of good and strong location provides the ease of the customers and suppliers to do business transaction and the means of going there is not a problem.

Reachable provides a link to buyers and customers at any given time without experiencing difficulty of making business transactions.

Comfortable provides the customers and buyers the feeling of being valued and develops loyalty and commitment on the process.

5.3 THE PRODUCT BRAND

Brand is an element that speaks for the product itself and its producer. Product brand is very important considering for it represents the total image of the company. Some large corporations create a position as brand manager who is responsible in taking care of the product despite that it incurs additional cost on their part. The main purpose of creating a brand manager is to give full attention to the product as it affects the name of the firm. Product brand projects positive or negative impressions to buyers as it brings promise or discontent to customers in terms of satisfaction. It is a mark considered as the most valuable asset of the company that dictates buyer's buying preference. People are accustomed to be brand conscious because it is their first consideration upon choosing a product. Pepsi Cola and Coca-Cola for example are almost identical in many ways but buyers mention their brand names respectively than naming them only as a soft drink.

How important is brand?

As discussed earlier, brand creates an image of trust to consumers and increases their loyalty as well. But how can a brand capture the heart of the buyers? Below summarizes the impact of brand to buyers:

- ✓ Brand conveys an assurance to customer's satisfaction.
- ✓ It promises to compel product performance.
- ✓ It brings impact to users identity and standing.
- ✓ It expresses good reputation.
- ✓ It is the firm's total identity.
- ✓ It promises guarantee.
- ✓ It serves as link between company and buyers.

A table that shows how brand helps a product make an identity

Product name	Focus	Promises
Addidas	Sports	Quality
Levis	Casual wear	Durability
Sony	Viewing	Clarity
San Miguel Beer	Drinking	Satisfaction
Apple Computer	Graphics design	Guarantee
Cellular Phones	Text & Call	Connection

Table 2 shows the aspect of brand identity

5.4 THE 4PS IN MARKETING

In marketing, firms understand that their product does not only make a sale by price alone it also comprises to complete the elements called 4Ps. This comes when the firm is able to establish a good positioning and branding. The underlying question in the implementation of the 4Ps requires a strategic planning. Below enumerate the different Ps in marketing.
1. Product
2. Price
3. Place
4. Promotion

The Product

This refers to goods and services offered for sale in the market. Products are tangible while services are intangible. Products such as pants, shoes, television, and computers give different satisfaction levels to users. Services on the other hand are intangible or physical attributes which cannot be seen such as doing a massage, driving a bus, or diagnosing a patient. Products and services are disparate yet they both provide satisfaction in a different manner. Buying food when one is hungry and being satisfied thereafter is similar to another who undergoes a massage and feels the pain relief after. Customer satisfaction is the best reward for any payment tendered.

Distinguishing product between services

Features

Product	Services
Tangible	Intangible
Warranty	Guarantee
Finished	Completed
Design	Style
Brand	Service type
Satisfaction	

Figure 1 shows the different features between product and services

The Price

In the general sense the term refers to the amount paid by customer in the course of buying the product. Product is composed of different features; however, price is the only element that provides revenue to the firm. It also determines the worth of a product. If the product is priced high this simply means that the quality and design target the class "A" buyers. A diamond can never be priced low since its nature and features are unique plus the scarcity of it. Price varies depending on the type of resources used in producing a unit of it. Pricing is crucial to every firm because it will determine the amount the product brings to it. Firm should make product differentiation so as to assign appropriate price associated with the quality and other features. There are different pricing schemes wherein entrepreneurs can use as shown below:
1. Cost -based pricing
2. Value- based pricing

Cost-based pricing

Is a firm pricing practice that simply adds a percentage from a product's total cost. The percentage of mark-up is determined by the firm on the basis of the production cost. If the firm wants to generate return on its investment (ROI) in the earliest possible time it can, however, due to growing competition and the presence of many identical products. Thus, determining the mark-up is not that easy. Through the percentage mark-up, the pricing approach is somewhat easy for the firm to determine its profit out the total revenue generated. A successful cost-based pricing practice suggests that the product does not have close or identical competition. The launching of Tondeña Rum whose price was marked up at 200 percent of the cost gave the firm an early return on investment; however, they experienced problem in sustaining the demand due to the growing number of competing products. To sustain the product, they just simply reduce the price as a sort of promotional strategy in order to continuously attract buyers. A simple illustration of cost-based pricing is shown below.

Sample of *Cost-based pricing approach*

Determining a unit cost of an item derives from computing the total cost and divided by the total output produced plus the determined percentage of mark up by the firm. To illustrate:

Input
(Variable cost)

Raw materials, Labor cost, advertising and promotion, Transportation, Salaries and allowances, Warehousing.
(Fixed cost)
Machine, land and building

Assuming that the combination of fixed and variable materials results to P 150.00 cost per unit and the determined mark-up is fifty percent, the selling price computation will be.

P 150.00 x 50%   = P 75.00
So, P 150.00 + 75.00

= P 225.00 is the selling price.

This pricing approach gives the firm an easy way of determining how much profit they are getting by just multiplying the number of unit sold times the price minus the mark-up considering it as a straight forward concept. Below illustrates the concept.

Assuming that at the end of the month the firm sells 2,500 units. The expected profit will be.

Total units sold   = 2,500
                   X 225.00

                   = 562,000.00 Gross sales

Expected profit is

2,500 units x 75.00 mark up

= 187,500.00 Firm's profit
(2,500 x 75.00)

If the firm wants to have an early return on investment (ROI) it should mark up the product up to 200 percent. The 200 percent is computed as the selling price times the mark up and the result will be.

The new selling price is 300 per unit.

To illustrate

Total units sold   = 2,500
                       X 300

                       = 759,000.00

Expected profit is

2,500 units x 150.00 mark up

= 375,000.00 Firm's profit
(2,500 x 150.00)

Value-based pricing

       This applies to the principle that as price is high; the presumption is that the quality is also high, whether this is true or not; value based-pricing concept appears this way. It can be achieved by knowing the rationale behind what the customers are willing to pay and how they perceive the value of the product. In value-based pricing, brand plays a very significant role. Consider this example. When a customer finds a low cost Levis brand at P300, it may be regarded as fake considering its original price. The value-based pricing concentrates on the value which customers are willing to spend their money with. This pricing approach is regarded as customer friendly since the value is the first consideration unlike cost-based pricing which is dependent on the firm's prerogative. Some firms apply the value-based pricing to attract more buyers. Low priced products with great value entice more customers but the firm sacrifices its profit generation. Price as an element that determines the value of a certain product varies according to firm' objectives.

5.5 PROMOTION

     As product is already available, to supplement its market acceptance and promotion is very important. Promotion is an act of communicating to customers the total product distinction. The sole intention for the firm is to persuade buyers to buy their product. This activity is costly especially on the part of the start-up business; hence, careful selection is needed prior

to choosing what promotional activity to use. There are many ways on promoting firm's product but what is important is to know the logic behind and using the guide questions will be beneficial. Below are the following guide questions.
1. Who are the key partners?
2. What are being promoted to satisfy them?
3. What is the target segment?
4. How can they be reached out?
5. How much will it cost?

Different ways to promote products
1. Advertising
2. Public relations
3. Social media
4. Direct selling
5. Selling through intermediaries

Advertising

It is a form of information drive to make people be aware of the presence of the products with an intention to persuade them to buy. Advertising helps the firm's product in many ways such as:
- ✓ Being aware of the product and capture interest in buying
- ✓ Emphasizing product uniqueness

This can be effectively used if the right choice of advertising medium is achieved. Most firms use radio as a medium of their advertisement to reach people even in far flung areas to inform them about the product. Advertising choices depending on what the firms intend to happen considering that varying products also need specific ways of advertising. To capture class A and B sectors, advertisers use television and newspapers to have an easy access to them who are more inclined to the said media. Advertising has some major shortcomings upon linking the products to people such as:
1. Its credibility
2. Its delivery
3. Its interest
4. Its cost
5. Its perception

Credibility is referred to being trusted or having good reputation. Choosing the right advertising arm is the top most consideration of the firm. In the Philippines today, the most trusted media outlet that performs with credibility is Bombo Radyo. It can be measured through the margin of listenership since it garners an outstanding loyalty of patronage.

Delivery is the clarity of the advertisement delivered to the audience which are the prospect customers. In some cases, firms use popular people to advertise product in order to have efficient advertising delivery.

Interest is the mode of arousing customer's value to the advertisement. People or buyers are interested to listen to fair than bias advertisement.

Cost is another factor that hinders advertisement. This is inherent to advertising whose cost does not give equal benefits.

Perception is the failure to connect to customers the real essence of advertising. The buyer feels that advertisement is somewhat fraudulent and he perceives things the other way.

Public relations

It is regarded as the most cost effective approach in advertisement where personal efforts aid in increasing awareness of the firm. Cost effective means that the activity is priceless unlike advertisement where contract of payment is made. In public relation, the firm is only required to maintain good image to the public and at the same time link to people. OISHI BOY, a Japanese restaurant just recently opened with limited resources. It has not used even a portion of advertisement out of their budget but has grown using effectively the public relation approach. They connect to friends and their friends also connect to some other friends. But most importantly, the bottom line that makes their public relation approach effective is "customer service". They don't sacrifice quality against price. Public relation is far better to other forms because advertising can be viewed as self-serving effort for the company. A simple illustration of public relation that links between people is shown below however, it must be noted that adopting this principle requires the heart of satisfying customers. Public relation starts when:
- ✓ maintaining a good reputation
- ✓ Establishing trust
- ✓ Delivering satisfaction

The public relation approach can be more understandable in the given illustration in figure 2 below.

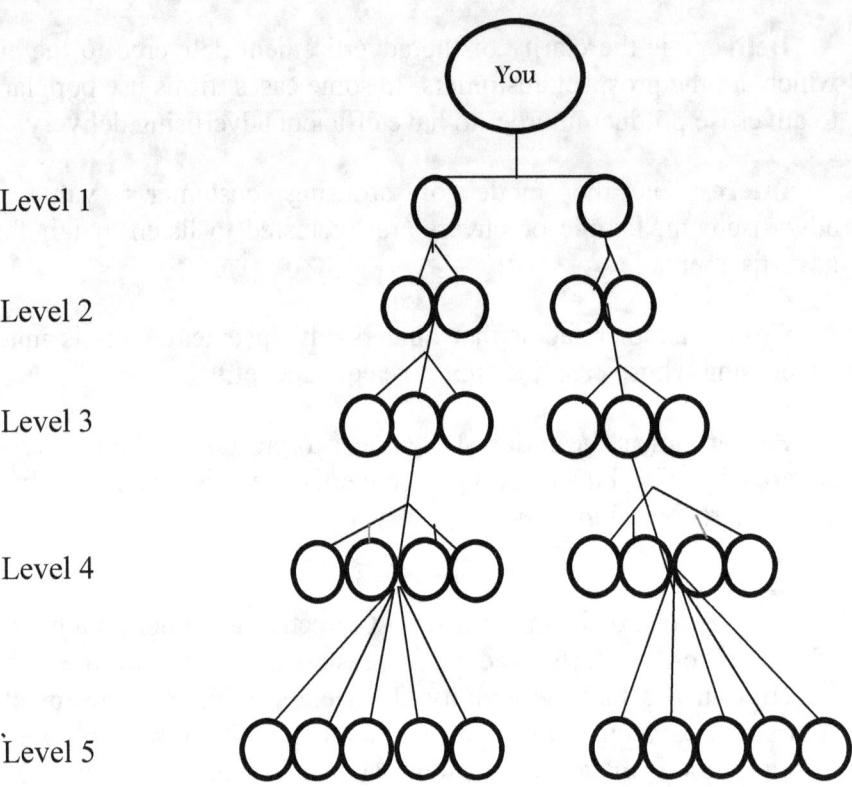

Figure 2 explains the model used to develop public relations

The public relation approach applies the principles of connecting to people. As it is said, it is the most cost efficient type of advertising medium. Although it is found to be very effective, its functionality in scope is limited. The above illustration explains that developing a public relations model starts with the key person. The model defines the so-called multiplier effect which means creating more potential buyers through a revelation of satisfied customers. Once a friend is satisfied by a proponent, he readily informs his friends about his experience. Like a chain of reaction, the satisfaction level can be shared to other parties. Then, as one shares, multiple of friends comes after the other. In every event, the number of guests gradually increases. These people can be from a circle of friends, classmates, church mates, office mates and people in the community who become friends and patronizers through good reputation.

Social media

As time changes, the evolution of technology like cell phones, iPod, tablet, lap top and the like is a big bang to people's lives and business. Advertising firms sometimes come and go due to the fast-paced technologies that flourish all over. In the earlier time, the dominant advertising tool aside from the tri-media was billboards. It is located in a very strategic location with a hope that it will increase product awareness. Most of the billboards use popular personalities as an added value to the effort of advertisement. These are traditional in scope; however, many firms still use this kind of advertising media for it is found to be effective as long as it is placed properly for public awareness. In the advent of social media, people are becoming more literate to the use and benefits of computer. People find more access using the computer especially using its most influential and controversial features like Facebook and Twitter. These media connect people extensively to all parts of the world. With just few seconds, two or more users are interconnected already. Businesses worldwide have greatly benefited on this regard. Their advertisement costs can be minimal or free. How can social media help in advertising? Posting pictures on the net allows families and friends to look into the celebrated affair and by chance the events will showcase some interesting parts that may answer some needs or introduce some new concepts. Interested parties may link to the event organizer or any concerned person and business starts. On the process, it gives benefit to the firm's product without experiencing advertising cost. Allowing people to advertise firm's product is a free of charge because they enjoy what they are doing, and for them it is just for fun in contrary, they are helping the firm with no extra cost.

Direct selling

It refers to the act of selling directly to prospect buyers. Firms make a sole control in distributing the product from its point of origin down to buyers without relying on the third party. Direct selling have both advantages and disadvantages. Below detail the following advantages and disadvantages:

Advantages
1. Selling directly to customers
2. Has the sole control over their product
3. Saves the cost of third party assistance

Disadvantages
1. Experience rental expenses for acquiring space

2. Allocates an amount for salaries to sales people
3. Maintenance

The present practices of direct selling are using technology to connect to potential buyers. This approach reduces the cost of the product considering that the business is no longer using middle men, distributors, wholesalers and dealers. A comparative approach between direct selling versus selling through the use of intermediaries is illustrated below.

Direct selling

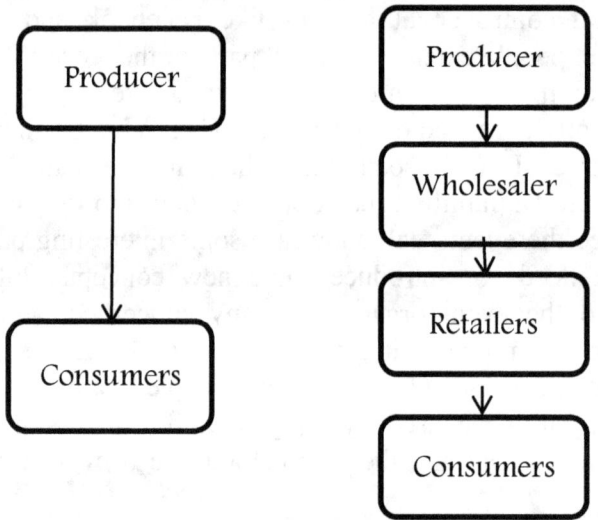

Figure 3 exhibits the difference between direct selling and selling through intermediaries

Selling through intermediarie

Selling through intermediaries is a typical business practice that remains to be very active at present business set up. It involves passing the entire firm's products to the wholesalers and distributors prior to the retail outlets. This selling approach brings different advantages and disadvantages to the firm.

Advantages
1. minimized task distribution .
2. Ease selling maintenance

3. No sales monitoring

Disadvantages
   1. Losses control over the product
   2. Losses the relationships to retailers
   3. Losses temporarily the product identity

Despite the above given advantages and disadvantages, some firms enter into an agreement of exclusive distributorships. This concept allows the distributors to do the selling activity. This activity can be an advantage to the firm for they will be able to generate volume of income generated from volume of production. For practical reasons, firms enter into exclusive distributors to be free of other overhead expenses. However, there are some advantages and disadvantages of this concept.

Advantages
   1. Firm easily gets revenue desired
   2. It relieves from burden in the maintenance of sales people
   3. Attention is focused only on production.

Disadvantages
   1. Has no direct control over the product
   2. Losses customer-dealer relationships
   3. Has no direct product feedback regarding the product

For a successful selling venture, it is a must that every firm understands the selling process by defining the sales process flow.

As cited from the concepts of PURLIFE U.K., a world renowned insurance company, the selling process is...

Step 1 **Prospecting**: Gathering information about the identified prospect

Step 2 **Making initial contact**: Taking some important details about the prospect

Step 3 **Qualifying the lead**: Determining the potential of the lead

Step 4 **Conduct sales presentations:** Presentation of product package and benefits

Step 5 **Address Objections and concerns:** Eradicating prospect doubts

Step 6 **Closing the sale**: Process the sales requirement and submit for approval

Step 7 **Follow-up:** Making an after sale service to clients

SUMMARY

1. Despite all odds and challenges in business, entrepreneurs undermine them all just to realize their opportunities. Their perseverance, faith and positive attitude matter a lot to succeed in their endeavour.
2. Managing business growth requires men and women to be active in finding some good positioning to ensure good returns as good market positioning promises achievable goals.
3. Segmentation is the key for every product. It is a process of matching products to potential market. It also classifies customers vis-a-vi the product use. Segmentation helps the firm on how to go about and provide them clear directions making the process effective.
4. There are different types of segmentation such as according to geographical location, demographics, and psychographics. All these elements attribute to firm's success.
5. Determining the target market is very important for the firm whether new or old for this will help to serve the market most efficiently. It is difficult for the firm to cater different types of market; hence, targeting specific one at a time will lead them to capture the market and yield some good result.
6. There are key activities that will lead the firm in their quest of making an effective marketing activity. One way of doing it is by way of answering the given questions in order for them to draw effective strategic plan that will answer the requirements of effective target marketing.
7. Brand by definition describes the product with its uniqueness and goodness. Most companies nowadays capitalize on hiring managers to focus on the products and protect them. The managers are responsible of making the product appealing and satisfying to users.
8. Product brand has several effects to customers that require the firm to be conscious enough. These effects are: assures customer satisfaction, compels product performance, brings impact to users identity and standing, expresses firms' reputation, gives the firm

total identity, promises guarantee, and serves as link between company and buyers.

9. There are four very important Ps in marketing. These include product, price, place and promotion. The four Ps are very important in the field of marketing as they represent the total component of the product. A product does not give meaning if the price is not attached to it, hence understanding the four Ps is a must to every firm.
10. Promotion is an activity that supplements its market acceptance and sales generation. It is a process of communicating to customers the total product distinction. Promotional activity is designed to persuade the buyer to buy. There are lots of guiding questions that will lead firms in maximizing the use of effective promotion such as who are the key partners, what are being promoted to satisfy them, what segment is used for targeting, how are targets be reached and how much will it cost.
11. Products can be promoted in different venues such as the use of advertising, public relations, social media, direct selling and intermediaries selling.
12. Advertising plays a vital role in marketing as it is the medium that makes people or buyers be aware of the product. The sole intention is to persuade buyers. Advertising is viewed to be effective but in some instances, they experience short comings in terms of credibility, delivery, interest, and perception.

DISCUSSION QUESTIONS

1. Why is managing growth important? What is the impact of growth mismanagement to the firm?
2. Does market positioning assure the firm favorable return? If so, in what instance? Discuss.
3. Discuss the elements of product segmentation. What are the benefits of the activity? Discuss on how to go about it?
4. Discuss the steps in the segmentation process and the important contribution of the activity to marketing?
5. What is the role of target market in the marketing activity? And why is it necessary? What is the firm trying to convey? Discuss.
6. Why is product positioning a challenge to every firm? Discuss your understanding to this statement "May the best firm win".

7. Why brand is considered the most important element of the product? What is the rationale behind why firm spends too much to protect the brand?
8. Discuss the hidden promise brought by brand?
9. In the 4 Ps of marketing, why is price important? Why is price inseparable to the product itself? Discuss.
10. Between cost-based pricing and value-based, which of them is more beneficial to the firm and why? Discuss.
11. Discuss the essence of promotion and the reason of the firm in using it until now.
12. Which of the different ways to promote a product found to be effective in these changing times? Cite one and discuss.
13. In what instance advertising experiences major short comings? What are the factors that influence them? Discuss
14. What is the most cost effective approach in advertising and how to go about it?
15. In marketing and making a sale, why is good prospecting important and what is it all about? Discuss

KEY TERMS (according to their appearance)

target market	**business enthusiast**	**business idea**
start-up competition	**segmentation**	**demographics**
geographics	**psychographics**	**business models**
prospecting	**positioning**	**brand**
promise guarantee	**inseparable**	**cost-based**
value- based	**credibility**	**perception**
multiplier effect	**social media**	**qualifying lead**

Works Cited

1. Anderson, Raymond. The Credit Scoring Toolkit: Theory and Practice for Retail Credit Risk Management and Decision Automation. Oxford: Oxford UP, 2007. Print.
2. Arya, Narendra. Social Media. New Delhi: Anmol Publications, 2011. Print.
3. Cartwright, Roger. Mastering Marketing Management. New York: Palgave, 2002. Print.
4. Espejo, Roman. Advertising. Detroit: Greenhaven, 2010. Print.

5. Grewal, Dhruv, and Michael Levy. Marketing. Boston: McGraw-Hill Irwin, 2010. Print.
6. Hammer, Sabine, and Christiane Schmeken. Promotion. Bielefeld: W. Bertelsmann, 2004. Print.
7. Hendrix, Jerry A. and Hayes Darrel C. Public Relation: Case-Based Approach. New Delhi: Cengage Learning India Private Limited, 2011. Print.
8. Kahn, Paul M. Credibility: Theory and Applications; Proceedings of the Berkeley Actuarial Research Conference on Credibility, Sept. 19-21, 1974, the Univ. of California, Berkeley. New York: Acad. Pr., 1975. Print.
9. Klussmann, Wolfram. Value Based Pricing Wertbasierte Preisfindung in Der Automobil- Und Nutzfahrzeugzulieferindustrie. München: AVM, 2012. Print.
10. Kotler, Philip, and Gary Armstrong. Principles of Marketing. Boston: Pearson Prentice Hall, 2012. Print.
11. Maund, Barry. Perception. Montréal: McGill-Queen's UP, 2003. Print.
12. McAndrew, John. Direct Selling: Dynamic Strategies, Stories and Techniques for Creating High Income through the Profession of Direct Selling. Hartwell, Vic.: Temple House and Sid Harta, 2003. Print.
13. Murdock, Steve H. Demographics: A Guide to Methods and Data Sources for Media, Business, and Government. Boulder, CO: Paradigm, 2006. Print.
14. Pogia, Michael. Target Market: An Investigation of the Relationship between Fine Art and Advertising. 2000. Print.
15. Ravenhill, Mark, and Mark Ravenhill. Product. London: Bloomsbury, 2013. Print.
16. Turner, William Henry. Market Positioning: A Research Approach for Higher Education. 1982. Print.
17. Wong, Monica. Fat Angelo's: Entrepreneurial Growth. Hong Kong: Centre for Asian Business Cases, the U of Hong Kong, 2003. Print.
18. R. Jones and J. Rowley, "Entrepreneurial Marketing in Small Business: A conceptual Exploration, Pearson/Prentice Hall, 2011.
19. P. Kotler, "Marketing Insights from A to Z, Concepts Every Manager Needs to Know", John Willey & Sons, 2009.
20. D. S Kennedy, "The Ultimate Marketing Plan", Adams Business, 2011.

21. N..J Hicks, "Branding Health Service Marketing", Aspen Publishers, 2000
22. L.E Boone and D. L Kurtz, "Contemporary Marketing" Cengage Learning, 2012.
23. P. Kotler and G. Armstrong, "Principles of Marketing", 13th edition, Prentice Hall, 2010.
24. B. Rosenbloom, "Marketing Channels", 8th edition, Cengage Learning, 2011.
25. C.W Lamb and C, McDaniel, "Essentials of Marketing", 7 editions, Cengage Learning, 2012.
26. R.D Smith, "Strategic Planning for Public Relations", 3rd edition, New York 2009.

INTERNET SITE ADDRESS

For definition of credibility, see, https://www.google.com.et/search

Chapter 6

DEVELOPING MARKET REASEARCH AND SALES FORECASTING

Introduction

As discussed primarily in the previous chapter, maintaining growth in business entails a lot of constraints and sacrifices. Some businesses may prosper, others may not. Success or failure in business depends largely on how equipped a business with such as a good plan, trained staff, strategies and linkages. In a competitive world, a business must not rely on its assets alone but it must keep abreast of the latest developments. Research is the answer. It is vital to any type of business ventures as it provides pertinent information beneficial to the business. The research efforts are focused on finding some possible business opportunities leading to expansion, modification and other development. It also enhances the capability not only of the management but all involved in business operations. Hence, the success in coming up with a research effort in marketing can be best achieved using the basic guidelines in identifying the key element of the task using some guide questions. The business model canvas designed by the "*U.C. Berkely Startups Competition*" provides the following guide to be considered in doing the research tasks.

1. What discoveries can help the firm?
2. What key activities do the tasks require?
3. What business problems must be discovered?
4. How important is this to business and customers?
5. What key resources are needed?

Using the above guide questions will lead the research team attain meaningful explorations for business advantage.

6.1 DOING THE MARKETING RESEARCH

Research activity is often a challenge to every business firm. The word research is somewhat common but the essence of it is very tremendous in terms of providing assistance to the firm on the basis of information gathering. The task cannot be denied that it entails a bigger portion of firm's financial budget allocation in doing this. Firms are always facing the challenge for this task; however, they cannot do away with this information gathering process as it helps them to sustain in business. Research also gives life to the business because some preventive measures can be done ahead using the advance data gathered in the course of the study. A research activity does not limit as to the size of the firm. Although this is expensive, some firms opt to use their internal researcher for practical reasons however, the result is somewhat limited. Most researches are designed to perform activities such as sales analysis, development of new product, assessment of advertising and sales forecasting. These are heavy requirements that require large firm to outsource researchers in order to provide the wider scope of information that cannot be done by their internal researchers. The famous research provider like Nielsen Company can assist in any information resources and many more.

Types of research

There are different types of research activities depending on what the firms want to discover. In marketing, types of research include:
1. Exploratory
2. Descriptive
3. Causal

Exploratory research
It is a process of investigation to identify problems or any situations with its causes and effects and other important related facts. The activity includes:
- Group discussion
- Interview
- Experiment

Descriptive research
A type of research that employs asking questions with the hope of acquiring accurate and appropriate answers. It mainly focuses on describing the characteristics of a population or a phenomenon being studied. This research process applies the mechanics of using structured questionnaires, structured interviews and data analysis.

Causal research
It refers to a research method involving the assessment of the cause and effect relationships. In business, causal research is very useful considering that it applies some tests to cases and events and predicts hypotheses.

6.2 THE MARKETING RESEARCH PROCESS

As discussed earlier, top management is dependent on the output of the research because from this information they can benchmark some possibilities of improvement during the planning stage. Information in this case is vital in providing valued information that will contribute to effective and timely planning and decision making. The marketing research process involves six steps namely:
1. Defining the problem
2. Conduct exploratory research
3. Formulate hypothesis
4. Create a research design
5. Collecting data
6. Interpret and present data

Defining the problem

Most often than not, problems need solution however, in some instance, they become more complicated considering that there is no appropriate solution provided and its wrongful definition. A problem definition is a process of knowing the cause and finding appropriate solution. Consider an illustrative example that guides management in defining the problem. Suppose a vegetable vendor losses 10 percent of their customers for the past 6 months. The loss of the customers is the problem and to define the problem, firm must look into the underlying cause of losing customers. The occurrence of the problem is always coupled with a cause behind it. Hence, problem definition requires knowing the cause behind a problem so that appropriate solution can be done. Below illustrates the process of defining a problem.

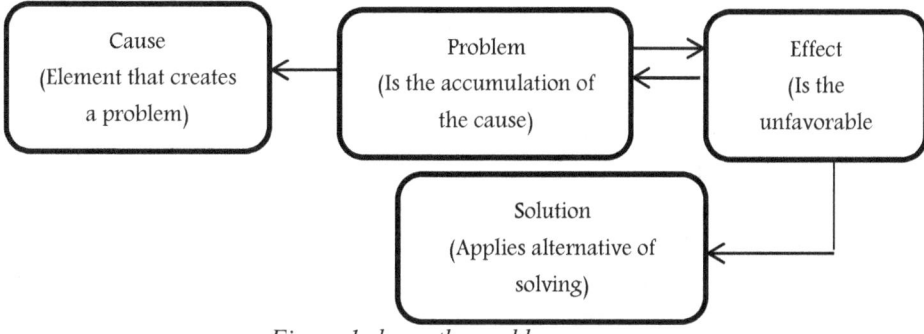

Figure 1 shows the problem process

As shown in the above diagram, problems are rooted from their causes. No problem happens without a cause; hence, the contributory factor to the problem is the cause itself. The problem now brings unfavorable effect or outcome that requires an appropriate solution. A suggested solution is not temporary in nature to avoid recurrence, it should be permanent.

Conduct exploratory research

Exploratory research can be effectively done when the firm is able to define the problem. This type of research concept seeks to find the cause of the problem and discuss the situation to top management and other research teams on the basis of the data gathered. Consider the above problem where the vegetable vendor losses about ten percent of his customers. Losing his customer is really a problem however, the cause is yet to determine. As research addresses this concern, the probable causes can be linked to pricing, competition, services, environment and the like. The problem can be treated as internal and external. The internal are those that come from within like behaviour and services while the external are those from outside like environment and competition. These are the potential sources that can be used in conducting an exploratory research.

Formulate hypothesis

The third step of the research process is legitimate to do after the previous two steps such as defining the problem and exploratory research are completed. Hypothesis is referred to an initial theory of findings for a specific event that deserves an explanation. It is a process of testing the relationship of an event either as null hypothesis or alternative hypothesis. For example, OISHI BOY restaurant noticed an increase of their number of customers. The researchers can make a hypothesis on the sudden increase of customers. The hypothetical guesses can be due to good services or quality of food. The hypothesis can be tested through:

Null hypothesis:
H_0: There is no significant relationship between good service and quality of food in the sudden increase of customers.

Alternative hypothesis
H_{01}: There is a significant relationship between good service and quality of food in the sudden increase of customers.

The hypothesis can be tested using different statistical tools to determine the appropriate findings. A negative finding or no significance rejects the hypothesis but if the result is significant or positive, it accepts the hypothesis. To understand further the implementation of formulating the hypothesis, consider the illustration below.

Sample problem

How do the customers of OISHI BOY compare their observations in terms of services considering age?

Data:	Group A (40 and below)	Group B (41 and above)
	3	14
	7	18
	10	19
	16	20
	17	20

Solution:

1. Null Hypothesis

H_0: There is no significant relationship between good service and quality of food in sudden increase of customers viewed according to age.

2. *Alternative hypothesis*

H_{01}: There is a significant relationship between good service and quality of food in sudden increase of customers according to age.

3. Test statistics
   $t = < tc$: Not Significant: Accept H_0
   $t > tc$: Significant: Reject H_0

4. Rejection Region (at 0.05 level of significance)
   $df = N_1 + N_2 - 2 = 5 + 5 - 2 = 8$
   From table --------(one tailed)
   $tc = 1.86$

5. Calculation of Test Statistics

   Group A   Group B
   (40 and below)   (41 and above)

X_1	X_1^2	X_2	X_2^2
3	9	14	196
7	49	18	324
10	100	19	361
16	256	20	400
18	324	20	400
54	738	91	1681

$$t = \frac{X_1 - X_2}{\sqrt{\dfrac{S_1^2}{N_1} + \dfrac{S_2^2}{N_2}}}$$

$$S^2 = \frac{\sum X^2 - \dfrac{(\sum X)^2}{N}}{N-1}$$

$$S_1^2 = \frac{738 - \dfrac{(54)^2}{5}}{5-1} \quad \text{and} \quad S_2^2 = \frac{1681 - \dfrac{(91)^2}{5}}{5-1}$$

$$= 38.7 \qquad\qquad = 6.2$$

Mean; $X_1 = \dfrac{54}{5}$

$= 10.8$ and

$X_2 = \dfrac{91}{5}$

$= 18.2$

Hence;

$$t = \frac{10.8 - 18.2}{\sqrt{\dfrac{38.7}{5} + \dfrac{6.2}{5}}}$$

t= **2.48**

6. Conclusion

Since the computed t is <tc, the null hypothesis is rejected, therefore there is a significant relationship between good service and quality of food served at OISHI BOY which contribute to the sudden increase of customer according to age.

Finding the value of "t", please refer to the table below labelled as "Values of t"

VALUES OF "t"

d.f.	Level of Significance for one-tailed test					
	.10	.05	.025	.ol	.005	.0005
	Level of Significance for two-tailed					
	.20	.10	.05	.02	.01	.001
1	3.078	6.314	12.706	32.821	63.657	636.619
2	1.886	2.920	4.303	6.965	9.925	31.958
3	1.638	2.353	3.182	4.541	5.854	12.941
4	1.533	2.132	2.776	3.747	4.604	8.610
5	1.476	2.015	2.571	3.365	4.032	6.859
6	1.440	1.943	2.447	3.143	3.707	5.959
7	1.415	1.895	2.365	2.998	3.499	5.405
8	1.397	1.860	2.306	2.896	3.355	5.041
9	1.383	1.833	2.262	2.821	3.250	4.781
10	1.372	1.812	2.228	2.764	3.169	4.587
11	1.363	1.796	2.201	2.718	3.106	4.437
12	1.356	1.782	2.179	2.681	3.055	4.318
13	1.350	1.771	2.160	2.650	3.01	4.221
14	1.345	1.761	2.145	2.624	2.977	4.140
15	1.341	1.753	2.131	2.602	2.947	4.075

Create a research design

The forth step in the research process is the creation of a research design. A research design serves as the master plan in conducting research activity. Researchers should see to it that the output of the research will provide the necessary facts to measure what is intended. A successful research is guided by proper selection of respondents. They are the instruments that contribute to the realization of a good research output. The credibility and reliability of the respondents are very important in the process considering that their responses will be the basis of answers to the problems set beforehand.. Since respondents contribute a very important role in the research efforts, they are selected on a random basis to ensure that they can provide genuine idea in response to the given questions.

Collecting data

The fifth step in the research process is collecting data. This is the output of floated questionnaires to the respondents. The collected data will be tallied and tabulated to determine the results. There are two forms of data that a researcher can use such as the primary and the secondary data. The *primary* data are those that are first-hand information gathered in the conduct of the research. The primary data are somewhat difficult to achieve since it requires more effort doing it. Considering that the information is new, it requires some validation process to make the data more reliable. Unlike the secondary data, these are available most often in the shelves or any published materials. The National Statistics Office is one of the reliable sources of information when a researcher wants to have information related to population.

Interpreting and presenting data

The last stage of the research process is the interpretation and presentation of data. In this phase, the researchers will analyse and imply the results. Based on the implications, the researchers can draw some appropriate recommendations. Findings and proposed recommendations will then be presented to top management for appropriate course of action. The final data should be in the form of a report citing therein the summary of research findings, recommendations and conclusions.

6.3 SALES FORECASTING

Any marketing activity faces a challenge in forecasting. Most firms do the forecasting every year depending on what is defined in their development plan. Sales forecasting activity carries a major role in business operations in terms of decision making considering that forecasting guides managers what to do, when to and how to do it. Forecasting on the other hand serves as the backbone of selling and marketing operations since it incorporates financial budget allocations. Poor management forecast will lead to business failure and overstated forecast will also lead to a negative impression to employees and the sales force as a whole.

What is forecasting?

In general sense, forecasting is a process of predicting possible future occurrence on the basis of the past information. It can also be defined as predicting some future outcomes using the past information. There are many definitions of the word forecasting however, what is important is to arrive at an appropriate figure. There are two types of forecast, namely:

1. ***Qualitative***: uses survey, opinions, and reports rather than acquiring the exact historical data.

2. ***Quantitative*** uses survey to determine such as the customer's taste, preferences, business projections and future conditions of the economy. This type of forecast uses some statistical validation to qualify results and findings. For further understanding, an illustration is given below.

Sample:

Forecasting based on ten years of sales summary

Year	Sales (in millions)	
1	65	
2	75	
3	90	
4	85	
5	75	
6	85	
7	95	
8	105	
9	65	
10	55	
11	= 75	(MA 3)
12	= 79.2	(MA 5)
13	= 79.9	(MA7)

From the given data the firm wants to forecast:

Year 11 using moving average 3 (MA3)
Year 12 using moving average 5 (MA5)
Year 13 using moving average 7 (MA7)

The general rule: count the number of the most recent information to determine the future forecast.

Solution:

MA 3 = 55 + 65 + 105 = 225/3 = **75**
MA 5 = 75 + 55 + 65 + 105 + 95 = 396/5 = **79.2**
MA 7 = 79.2 + 75 + 55 + 65 + 105 + 95 + 85 = 559.2/7 = **79.9**

The purpose of forecasting is to determine the closest figure that the sales person is expected to deliver to the firm. A forecast does not mean to be exact however, it will only guide the sales person as basis in finding strategies to achieve it. The delivery of the certain forecasted figure either exact, beyond or less is most likely influenced by time; hence, good forecasting should consider time as variable. Forecasting as an effective marketing tool can help the firm and sales force in many ways. There are favorable and unfavorable outcomes may happen among the firm, the business and the sales force in giving a forecast beyond it as viewed below.

Favorable to:

Firm

- ✓ Giving a forecast beyond it brings more revenues than what is expected.
- ✓ Making production people more active for continuous processing of inventory requirements.
- ✓ It is a sort of confidence building on their part for having sign of growth
- ✓ It prevents entry of competing product since there is an available supply.

Business

- ✓ It hedges them from experiencing stock shortage because sales person can make extension of volume orders to customer.
- ✓ Can cater more customers because of product availability.

- ✓ Can capture more loyal customers due to some business consideration like credit extensions.
- ✓ Giving them the leverage of time upon taking an order.

Sales person

- ✓ Giving them the additional income especially those on commission basis.
- ✓ Extends the frequency of customer calls because they adjust consumption volume to their clients.
- ✓ Can extend area coverage due to the extension of visit frequency.
- ✓ Can persuade customers to sell priory the company's products versus their competitors' on the condition of giving them incentives.

Unfavorable

The above strategy of giving beyond sales forecast it is noted to have the same benefit experiences to the firm, business and sales persons. However, an unfavorable occurrence might appear if the sales people are not vigilant in monitoring customers. More products extended beyond normal to the customers are crucial for the firm in terms of managing finances which may affect revenue generation.

6.4 TECHNIQUES IN FORECASTING

Forecasting is always a requirement in business and sales in particular considering that the manager and the firm want to project good monetary and physical sales volume. Forecasting helps the firm in many ways since it will aid them in achieving such plan of activity with the use of different techniques. There are two techniques frequently used in forecasting, the qualitative and quantitative. The two popular forecasting techniques embraced different sub-areas to use as shown below.

Qualitative
- Top management's role of thumb
- Delphi technique
- Knowledge of sales force
- Survey of buyers' objectives

Quantitative
- Test marketing

- Trend analysis
- Exponential smoothing

Top management's role of thumb
The term called top management's role of thumb is based on the management's actual observation in the field. The basis for this kind of technique can be generated through an accumulated report of the middle managers by weekly, monthly, quarterly and even annually. From this information they can make a forecast as to how much possible figure the firm will generate for a certain period. This can be effective and easy for them to do however, there are some limitations and can only be effective in short run.

Delphi technique
This approach has a similarity to the top management's role of thumb since they use some experts to do the survey using questionnaires. The only difference in this approach is it is time consuming considering that the data generated by the experts must be validated.

Knowledge of sales force
This approach is done purely by using the knowledge of sales force believing that they are the masters of their own territory. The process involves collecting information of different sales levels to come up an aggregate results then design for a forecast. This approach however is found to have some limitations considering that the concerned salespeople would likely to be conservative considering that this is the basis for determining sales quota. Some sales people when asked about the figure are hesitant to tell instead to play safe. They well give what they feel they can deliver only. However, without hesitations by sales people, these kinds of technique are believed to be the best among others.

Survey of buyer's objectives
The process involves asking customers through a survey questionnaire, phone calls, mails, personal interview and feedback mechanisms to determine their purchase intentions. This approach is considered to be less effective considering that the customers' responses cannot be translated to actual purchase at all times. This approach may help the firm in predicting in a short run however, it is somewhat expensive.

Test marketing

This is an experimental approach of knowing and gauging the customer's response to new product offerings. This testing activity also helps the firm by observing varying product pricing and generates ideas about alternative advertising and promotions to supplement the product. The test marketing is usually done in places where there are lots of people such as malls where pre-selling can be done.

Trend analysis

This forecasting technique of trend analysis uses historical sales and time relationships. Trend can be effectively used if the past information is available. The approach uses some sales patterns as basis for forecasting future events. It is also a process of observing sales performance for a number of years. The percentage growth of 15 for three years for example can be a potential addition to next year's forecast.

Exponential smoothing

This approach in forecasting is regarded as the most sophisticated considering that weights are assigned to determine the forecast. The most recent annual sales performance of the firm is given weight as basis for determining a forecast. This kind of statistical technique is the most common tool in quantitative forecasting.

SUMMARY

1. To be well-informed of what is going on out the business arena; firm should require some research activities. Research enhances the capability not only of the management but to all involved in business operations. The success of every business endeavour cannot be done by one person alone so concerted effort is required so that the goals and prosperity are attained. The success in coming up with a research effort in marketing can best achieved using the basic guidelines in identifying the key element of the task using some guide questions.
2. Research activity is often a challenge to every business firm. The word research is somewhat common but the essence of it is very tremendous in terms of providing assistance to the firm on the basis of information gathering. The task cannot be denied that it entails a bigger portion of firm's financial budget allocation in doing it. Firms

are always facing the challenge for this task however, they cannot do away with this information gathering process as it helps them to sustain in business. Research also gives life to the business because some preventive measures can be done ahead using the advance data gathered in the course of the study.

3. A research activity does not limit as to the size of the firm. Although it is expensive, some firms opt to use their internal researcher for practical reasons however, the result is somewhat limited. Most researches are designed to perform activities such as sales analysis, development of new product, assessment of advertising and sales forecasting. These are heavy requirements that require large firms to outsource researchers in order to provide the wider scope of information that cannot be done by their internal researchers.

4. Effective research can be gleaned clearly if the process is done well. The output can be used to benchmark some possibilities of improvement during the planning stage. More so, the information is vital in providing valued information that will contribute to effective and timely planning and decision making.

5. Most often than not, problems require solution however, it sometimes worsens due to no appropriate solution or it can be because of wrongful definition.

6. A problem definition is a process of knowing the cause and finding an appropriate solution. Some illustrative examples are given to guide the management in defining the problem. The exploratory research can be effectively done when the firm is able to define the problem. This type of research concept seeks to find the cause of the problem and discuss the situation to top management and other research teams on the basis of the data gathered. Consider the problem when the vegetable vendor losses about ten percent of his customers. Losing his customers is really a problem however, the cause is yet to be determined.

7. The probable causes affecting loss of customers can be attributed to some factors like pricing, competition, services, and environment. The output of the research will serve as basis for improvement and pointers for planning stage.

8. The problems can be treated as internal and external. The internal are those that come from within like behaviour and services while the external are those from outside like environment and competition. These are the potential sources that can be used in conducting an exploratory research.

9. The third step of the research process is legitimate to do after the previous two steps such as defining the problem and exploratory research are completed. Hypothesis is referred to an initial theory of findings for a specific event that deserve an explanation.
10. The fourth step in the research process is the creation of a research design. A research design serves as the master plan in conducting research activity. Researchers should see to it that the output of the research will provide the necessary facts to measure what is intended.
11. A successful research is guided by proper selection of respondents. They are the instruments that contribute to the realization of good research output. The credibility and reliability of the respondents are very important in the process considering that their responses to the questionnaires will create an impact to the research findings. Since respondents contribute a very important role in the research efforts, they are selected on a random basis to ensure that they can provide genuine idea in response to the given questions.
12. The sixth step in the research process is collecting data. This is an output of the floated questionnaires to the respondents. The collected data will be tallied and tabulated to determine the result. There are two forms of data that a researcher can use such as the primary and the secondary data. The *primary* data are those first-hand information gathered in the conduct of the research. They are somewhat difficult to achieve since it requires more effort in doing it. Considering that the information is new, it requires some validation process to make the data more reliable. Unlike the secondary data, these are available most often in the shelves or those published materials.
13. The last stage of the research process is the presentation and interpretation of data. From the results, the researchers will imply, make conclusions and appropriate recommendations. Findings and proposed recommendations will be presented to the top management for appropriate course of action.
14. Forecasting is a process of predicting possible future occurrence on the basis of the past information. It can also be defined as predicting some future outcomes using the past information.
15. Forecasting is always a requirement in business and sales in particular considering that the manager and the firm want to project some realistic monetary and physical sales volume. Forecasting helps the firm in many ways since it will aid them in achieving such plan of activity with the use of different techniques.

DISCUSSION QUESTIONS

1. What are the key elements contributed by research to the firm? Discuss.
2. Why do most firms consider research as a way of giving life to business? Discuss.
3. Which type of research enumerated in this chapter considered as the most effective and why? Discuss.
4. Discuss the principle, "There is no problem without a cause". Discuss each element.
5. Why is hypothesis necessary in conducting research? What is its contribution to the attainment of research output?
6. What is a research design and its processes? Discuss.
7. Why is forecasting necessary for the firm? What are the elements of good forecasting? Discuss each of them.
8. What is the difference between qualitative and quantitative forecast? Discuss.
9. Enumerate some benefits forecasting bring? Discuss each of them.
10. Is beyond forecasting giving the same benefits to firms, salespeople and business? If so, give some limitations to each of them.
11. Is the role of thumb forecasting techniques applicable to the present times? Discuss and support your answer.
12. Pre-selling is also called test market. Is this approach still effective in these modern times? Discuss.

KEY TERMS (in order of their appearance

Start-up	preventive measures	exploratory descriptive
Causal	null hypothesis	rejection region qualitative
Quantitative	moving average	**Delphi techniques**
exponential smoothing		

Works cited

1. Barton, John. *Hypothesis: Poems*. Toronto: House of Anansi, 2001. Print.
2. Birn, Robin, and Patrick Forsyth. *Market Research*. Oxford: Capstone Pub., 2002. Print.
3. Chi, Keon S. *State Legislator Compensation: A Trend Analysis*. Lexington, KY: Council of State Governments, 2006. Print.

4. Dalrymple, Douglas J., and Leonard J. Parsons. *Basic Marketing Management*. New York: Wiley, 2000. Print.
5. Donoghue, Martine, and Peter H. Mann. *Public Library Statistics 1977-1987: A Trend Analysis*. Loughborough: Library and Information Statistics Unit, Dept. of Library and Information Studies, Loughborough U, 1988. Print.
6. Fildes, Robert, and P. Geoffrey Allen. *Forecasting*. Los Angeles, CA: SAGE, 2011. Print.
7. Good, Phillip I., and James W. Hardin. *Common Errors in Statistics (and How to Avoid Them)*. Hoboken, NJ: Wiley, 2006. Print.
8. Hosokawa, Kōmei. *The Yawuru Language of West Kimberley: A Meaning-based Description*. München: LINCOM EUROPA, 2011. Print.
9. Olsen, Wendy Kay. *Data Collection: Key Debates and Methods in Social Research*. London: SAGE, 2012. Print.
10. Riscinto-Kozub, Kristen A. *Effects of Service Recovery Satisfaction on Customer Loyalty and Future: An Exploratory ..* Place of Publication Not Identified: Proquest, Umi Dissertatio, 2011. Print.
11. Rose, Arthur P. *An Illustrated History of the Counties of Rock and Pipestone, Minnesota*. Salem, MA: Higginson Book, 1998. Print.
12. Salkind, Neil J., and Kristin Rasmussen. *Encyclopedia of Measurement and Statistics*. Thousand Oaks, CA: SAGE Publications, 2007. Print.
13. Tooley-Knoblett, Dian, and David W. Gruning. *Sales*. Eagan, MN: West, 2012. Print.
14. Vaus, D.A De. *Research Design*. London: SAGE, 2006. Print.
15. L. E. Boone, "Principles of Marketing", Cengage Learning Asia Pte ltd., 2013
16. D.A Shepherd and H. Patzelt, "The New Field of Sustainable Entrepreneurship, 2011.
17. C.-J Wang, L,-Wu, "Team Members Commitment and Start-up", Journal of Business Research, 2011.
18. G.T Lumpkin, "From Legitimacy to Impact: How Entrepreneurships Informs Life, Entrepreneurship Journal, 2011.
19. Salas, Vincent, "Statistics A Reviewer Text, 1998

INTERNET SITE ADDRESSES
For identification of type of research, see,
www://teachingcommons.cdl/cdip/faculty research
For definition of market research, see, *http://whatismarketresearch.com.*

CHAPTER 7

THE INDUSTRY
(COMPETITOR ANALYSIS AND SOCIAL RESPONSIBILITY)

Introduction

We are done with the research activity that guides the firm in their efforts towards achieving success. This chapter will analyse the industry versus the competitor and its rule to the society. No one can tell if he is strong or not until such time one discovers something in him not found in others. Eric, Mocca and Ahleen were both working at Tachibana restaurant a well-known Japanese restaurant with different specialization. Eric was known to be the Chef, Mocca in marketing and Ahleen was in customer service. They both leave the firm for they want to venture something of their own but it take sometimes before it happens.
In one vacation time about five years after, they group together and have a discussion over a cup of coffee regarding their plan of putting up a restaurant of their own. They are banking on their skills and experience on that business and have the confidence that it will be materialized. Last December 2014, they finally open the restaurant despite knowing that the location was surrounded with variety of food chain. When they are about to open, they learned that there is one of the same business venture is about to open but prior to their opening, the try eating at the OISHI BOY, the name of the restaurant and after eating, they only notice that they did not push though their schedule in opening their business. In this chapter, we will discuss and define industry analysis, competitor analysis, the industry, and social responsibility. *Industry analysis* is referred to as instrument that guides firms understanding about their position over other firm produces similar product or services. Good position could be a competitive edge of the firm that need to be capitalized. *Competitor analysis* is a process that determines what the competitor strength is and weaknesses that can be used as point of reference to draw a strategic offensive and defensive activity that identifies threats and opportunities. *Industry* is generally represented by business that offers similar product or services. In the case of restaurant business, these are those who cater to different classes of customers such as pre-cooked orders, ready to eat foods and the like. On the other hand, *social responsibility* is referred to ethical standards that one should adopt to maintain and uplift the balance between society and the economy

INDUSTRY ANALYSIS

For an effective industry analysis, it is suggested that the firm should be guided with some business models to understand the value proposition and answer questions leading to finding realistic approach in problem solving such as (1) is the location ideal for the chosen business? This means that, are there potentials (the traffic, the environment, people, industry around that be pointed as customers, (2) is the firm ready to face challenge? (3) Is there a possibility that the firm will experience some unfavorable circumstances in the course of doing business? Knowing this is very important for business to position in a very strategic location for this will bring them into a greater height if they will be able to maintain and sustain the quality of their product and services. Business is like deciding to take a dive in the pool but prior doing it; you have to check the deepness of it. As discussed earlier in the previous chapter, to be strong enough in business, we must first be familiar with the environment we are in and how business performs hence' studying the trends are very essential for the business to survive. There are three types of trend that firm needs to know namely:

- Environment trend
- Business trend
- Political trend

Economic trends

Economic trend is a must for entrepreneurs to know considering that this will harm the business operation by not getting aware of it. As it is said that what is certain in this world is change. An economic trend can be favorable or unfavorable hence; vigilance is needed and it is recommended that an alternative course of action is ready at any given time. Consider this example, during the past years, people using cars as a means of transportation. As years moving onwards and the number of car users increases, gradually motorist finds difficulty to find a parking area in the city. Added on to the problem is the government policy that requires car owners to provide their own parking area so that they cannot violate traffic ordinance. For that instance, motorist find solution to the problem by shifting to smaller type of vehicle that give opportunity to small type vehicle producers and affect the other. In the case of the restaurant business as cited in this chapter, an economic trend comes in many ways. The increasing number of competitor is one of the factors; stagnation of the recipe is also a factor, the possibility of losing employment that reduces disposable income of households, the possible entry of big and well-known food chain and many more are economic trend that every firm should know. In the Philippines, the sudden stoppages of the operation of the National Steel Corporation greatly affect the nearby firms and including the whole city. The closure results to deprivation of earning an economic benefit for the firm regardless of size including government. Businesses were affected in terms of profit while the government in terms of taxes. The said closure brings equal impact to both business and government as business sector finds difficulty to adjust the situation and the government finds difficulty also in meeting and delivering the basic social services needed which is inherent to them. These are the elements of economics trends that people in the business sector should be aware of.

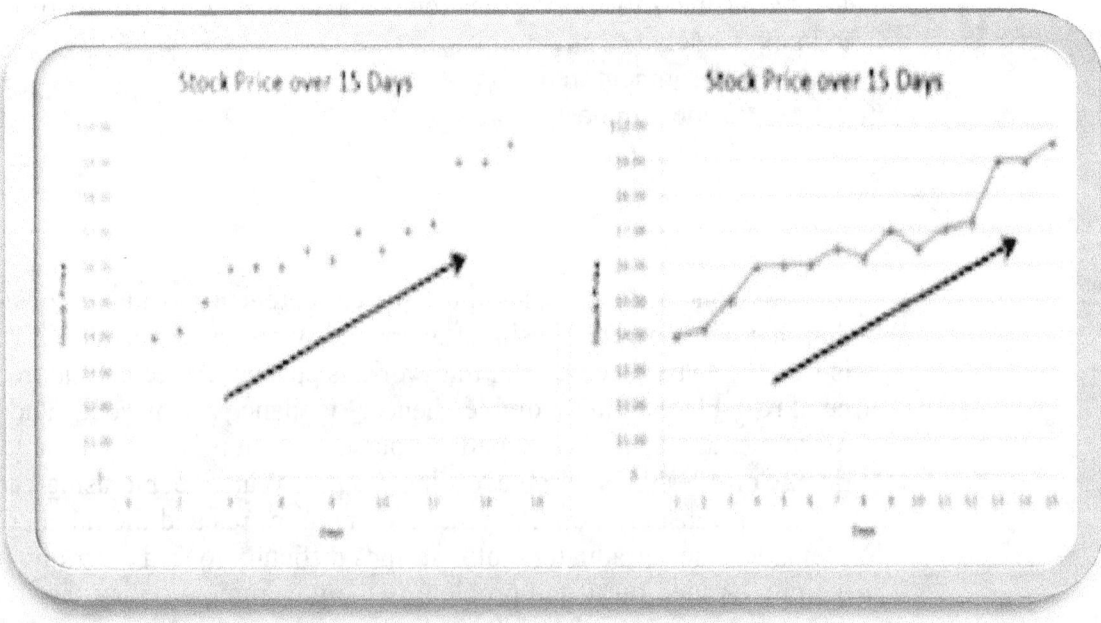

Figure 1 shows an example of trend. Source http://www.google.com.

Business trend

Business competes in different ways considering that the firm will always find ways how to survive. They will continue searching for some possibilities of generating favorable revenue. Business trend is another factor that for layman understands did not bring an impact to business. For example, large corporation expand their production site to places where the cost of labor is lower and making their product more competitive in terms of price because of lower production cost. In this case firm did not share similar advantage. The value proposition and the revenue stream in this case are somewhat unfair. In the advent of technology today, some businesses prosper by eliminating major components in the production such as carrying of inventories. They do business using on line successfully and increases their revenue generation through a reduction of operating cost.

Political trend

Another factor to consider in industry analysis for this will contribute unfavorable effect to business. Businesses are govern with certain rules and regulation implemented by the government. In the case of political trend, some business suffers due to strong political interventions. The mall political practices discourage business owners due to unfair government practices.

IDENTIFYING BUSINESS THREATS

Establishing any forms of business always face challenge regardless of its nature and capitalization. Small business such as an ordinary sari-sari store is not exempted to experience the same competition as large businesses do. Competition is always there considering that all business enthusiast will always take advantage of gaining at least a marginal return of the amount invested. There are different types of competition activity that make it as threat to every business however; these can be prevented by using a business model that guide entrepreneur's in overcoming them by answering the following questions such as:
1. What strategic preparation do we have to overcome them?
2. Which of the following business threat can directly affect our business?
3. What resources we need to address them? Below enumerate some of the business threats:
    - Product substitutes
    - New entrants
    - Rivalry among firms
    - Suppliers bargaining power

- Buyers bargaining power

Product substitute

The closer the product substitute to the main product is likely to create some chaos to them considering that the small difference wold triggers consumer to shift to product substitutes. On the hand, if the threat of substitute is not that strong, it would mean attractive to the main product. Consider going to places for a vacation and taking a hotel to have some rest and pay higher price because there is no other alternative choices such inn and lodging houses. The main business comfortably earned more profit since there is no such substitute for hotel. However, if the substitutes are available, the hotel now will create something extraordinary that the substitute do not have just to keep their customers with them. Most practices hotels adopt that is not available in some substitutes just like offering a free breakfast as package for room rates, amenities such as the use of swimming pool and other fitness gym for free. In the case of restaurant in keeping their customers aside from the quality and tasty foods, they give some extra package to delight customer and keep them coming back such as providing them free dessert and soup. Another example of substitutes can be experience between some service couriers like LBC, FedEx for cargo and packages, MLhuilier, Cebuana and many more for sending money. The threat that they experience is measured on time. Who among them can deliver the item fist and safe always the preferred choice of customers hence; firms do not the full control over their customers due to the presence of closed substitutes. Below illustrates the factors contributed to product or services due to substitutes.

Reason for shifting mode from the main product to substitutes and vice versa.

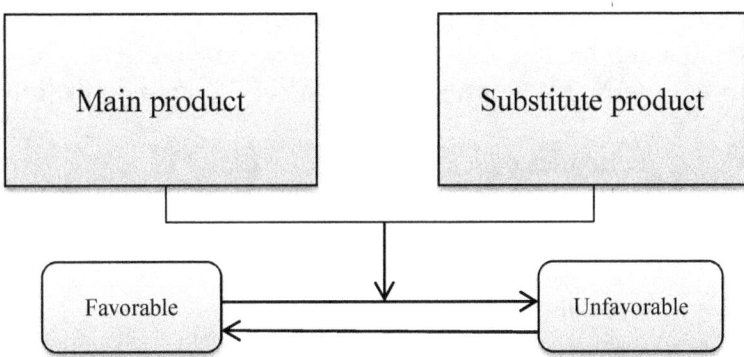

Figure 2 shows the interaction of customer shifting due to closed product substitutes

- If the price of the main product is high, customer shift to product substitute
- If the time of delivery takes longer by the substitute product, shifting can be done in favour of the main product.
- If the assurance is noted to be present to the substitute product, shifting can be favorable to substitute.
- If ambiance is present to the main product, shifting to the main product surely happen. The above illustration expresses the shifting mode to appear to product that has close substitutes making them a threat if not associated with attending customers need.

Threat to new entrants

The entry of a new firm in the industry brings favorable and unfavorable impressions to the business activity. A business without competition has a lesser chances of creating some improvements hence; entry of the new player becomes favorable for this will create an initiative to firm owners to make some improvement in many ways. On the other hand, this new entrants can bring unfavorable impact to the existing businesses if they are outweigh in terms of product offerings. Consider the entry of Ayala specifically in Cagayan de Oro City, a widely known business that design a unique industry model. It provides all services covering a wide variety of grocery lines, household items, RTW's, food chain, recreation of different kinds, wide parking space, outsourcing business, banking, hotel and many more, making the mall a one stop shop. Prior its official entry in the city, the good thing that happen to existing businesses are finding some improvements showing their customer that they are competent enough to exist in business despite new and famous one is coming. It could be advantageous for the existing business if the entry of the new player do not bring major turn out of the existing businesses however; this can be controlled if the firm has to do something in blocking the new entrants by putting some barriers. This barrier hinders the new entrant if the existing firm will be able to do the following activity to wit;

- Economies of scale
- Product differentiation
- Capital strength
- Cost
- Accessibility
- Legal requirements

The enumerated elements of blocking the entry of the new player can be best described using the model shown below.

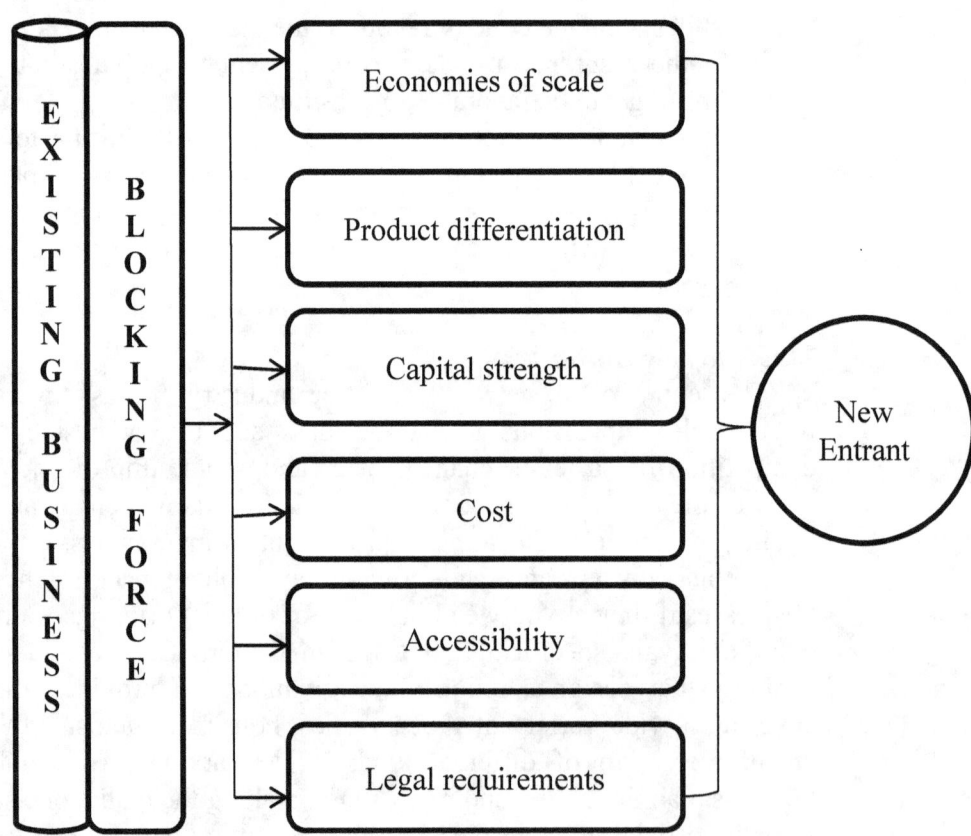

106

Figure 3 shows the blocking entry for new business

Economies of scale

Is a process of creating and maximizing firm competitive advantage over the new entrants. For example. San Miguel Corporation a world renowned beer maker and has a centennial dominance in the market of beer created different product lines to position in different market segment. With this kind of strategy, the firm is not easily bothered with new firm entering in the industry because of the wide variety of product that are already positioned to different target market. The economies of scale are firm's strategy that applies the activity of producing more products with a lesser cost. Large Corporation often experience the presence of the new entrant however; new players finds it hard to penetrate and capture their existing market share. Coca Cola, Pepsi and Nestle Corporation are among the large firm that is known to have practicing the economies of scale.

Product differentiation

The term denotes keeping firm's product intensively unique from others. The concept of product differentiation is innovation. Innovation is a continuing process of creativity making a strong consumers patronage. In the Philippines for example and talking about cell phones, there are variety of brands and models. In order for the product to be differentiated, firms create some feature of it not found to some other competing products. This is done by the firm not only to keep their existing customers and capture nee ones but to block competitors.

Capital strength

The capital requirement is another blockage that hinder new firm to enter in the market. For example, entering in Gasoline dealership requires large amount of financial capital over and above the necessary compliance.

Cost

This is referred to amount incurred in finding and acquiring property to be used in establishing a new business, considered as blockage for them. The increasing price of property such as land and equipment most of time discourage new entrant since acquiring them reduces their working capital requirements.

Accessibility

It is a given fact that existing businesses occupies a large portion of the display for example in the malls. Having additional new product, the probability in terms of creating space to be displayed on a strategic location is not a guarantee.

Legal requirements

Most of the times, new business player experience difficulty in entering the new business because of the legal requirement imposed by the government such as copy rights, patents, and trademarks. Meeting all the legal requirements some time reduces the interest of the new player to enter into the market.

Rivalry of the firm

Rivalry is inevitable as it is always the bottom line of every business. Rivalry affects some business alike up to the extent of price wars. Price war is not a healthy competition practice for business however; due to the presence of close substitute products, firm tend to reduce price and lowers down their percentage of revenue. Products where competition is not that intense would likely to earn more than product with closed substitutes. Close substitute's means that in the absence of the main product gives assurance to the substitute product as buyer's preference. Observing the market today and considering that there are lot of product with close substitutes, cell phones for example, dealers cannot make a bigger mark-up for the item because of many available dealers that sells identical product. Their ultimate strategy is to sell more units despite of lesser percentage of mark-up, at the end of the day, the volume of unit sold accounts for a bigger profit. Rivalry is not only experience in business however; in every walk of live, rivalry is always there. There are different ways in measuring the degree of rivalry among firms. Below enumerate some.
1. The degree of competition
2. The degree of differentiation
3. The degree of growth indicators
4. The degree of fixed cost requirements

The degree of competition

The presence of more competitors in similar market is more likely that one or more will initiate to lower down their price to attract buyers. Although the practice itself is not recommended however; for the business to survive, some strategy should be initiated by the firm. Common practices by firms in similar market use the so-called "fast moving product, reduced price". This means that firms observes which product is frequently purchased by buyers, then firms reduces its price to create an impression that he's price is low compared to others. This is one of the strategies that most competing firms are doing but other commodity is priced beyond normal. Accounting this strategy, the firm still earns and keep their loyal buyers.

The degree of differentiation

The higher the degree of product differentiation creates a strong rivalry however; those firms that sell identical products or services such as LBC and FedEx often compete on price. Their rivalry does not give meaning since the business nature has no significant differences.

The degree of growth indicators

This is referred to fast growing company that already achieved the level of stability in terms of patronage. Price reduction is less likely to happen since they already have enough customers for their products. Unlike other firms such those who are selling pre-need products strives a lot to gain bigger market share.

The degree of fixed cost requirements

Firm's that use sophisticated fixed cost such as modern machines and high cost of acquisition of property normally price their product higher. This is done in order to meet their expected return of investment (ROI) in a shorter time. After attaining the determined return on firm can make some possible adjustment such as price reduction as a means of keeping customers.

Suppliers bargaining power

This is referring to buyer and suppliers relationships. Most often, businessmen observes how buyers react to its product price. Noticed that when buyer feels that the price offer by the firm of the same quantity is higher than that of the others, shifting is more likely to happen. Buyers have strong influence to the price offered by supplier due to the presence of competitors. The strong influences of buyers will supressed the profit generation of the sellers. There are enumerated ways that suppliers should do to sustain profit generation and experience less pressure for buyers. Below name some of these.

1. Supplier focus

2. Cost standing
3. Number of substitutes

Supplier focus

A process that determines the number of sellers available in the market that sells identical products. Generally speaking, few sellers could be an advantage considering that this will reduce buyers influence to the price.

Cost standing

The acquisition cost of an item triggers buyers to switch to other suppliers however; this involve time and effort on the part of the buyers. The fewer the number of sellers of identical product and the cost of acquiring is almost at par, reduces the degree of byers switching to other suppliers.

Number of substitutes

Availability of close product substitutes are factors that affect the sellers and prompted them to reduce price and supresses their profit and revenue generation. The fewer the product substitute is advantageous to sellers considering that the influence of byers to the price is low. Consider if there is only one producer of anti-biotic medicine whose effectiveness is twice as good as those of substitute product, the seller of the product will not be affected by the substitute around however; continues selling and keeping the price high and in return continue to generate more revenue out of it.

Buyers bargaining power

Business is always represented by sellers and buyers; sellers sells, buyers consume. The buyers bargaining power arise and suppress the profit for the industry when they demand for better product quality to the firm at a lower cost. For example. A furniture manufacturing use ordinary material for their product and once it was sold to the market, buyers pointed out some negative comments regarding the quality and prompted producers to do some innovation to satisfy customer's need. The innovation entail using higher quality of material thereby reducing the profit margin of the firm. Another example of bargaining power of buyer is the government procurement system. Government when buying product to suppliers quoted their price and undergo a bidding process. The only way to qualify as supplier to the government is winning through lowest bid. The process will reduce the profit of the industry as supplier because of the strong influence of the buyer. There are some barriers that buyers find difficulty in influencing suppliers and suppress the profitability.

1. Number of buyers
2. Price
3. Product uniqueness

Number of buyers

The presence of fewer numbers of large buyers buying from large number of suppliers, influence to the price is likely to be less.

Price

Price is the determinant of an item. The higher the price reduces the quantity of volume sold in general sense however; the degree of importance that the buyer has to the product, the higher is the buyer sensitivity. For example, if the price sold by the supplier will affect a greater portion of his profit, the higher is the bargaining effort of buyer just to get the best price.

Product uniqueness

The greater is the product uniqueness over other suppliers, reduces the influence of buyers to the price. For example. Supplier A is the only seller to the product although there are other substitutes available however; the components parts, design and the appearance differ, buyers has lesser influence making a price reduction.

ANALYZING COMPETITIOR

Competitors are major elements that affect every business towards achieving goals hence it is very important for the firm to analyse and understand the direction and identify market with which to compete. Competitor analysis is a detailed flat form that defines the degree of competition. It guides the firm in identifying some effective ways of knowing the positions of their competitors and from then, finding how to gain competitive advantage. This is very important aspect especially to those new ventures entering into a very competitive nature of business. In the case of OISHI BOY restaurant, they already identified their competitor hence; finding strategy to keep their customer is already define and one way of competing is making their product unique and continues to create some new recipe that will delight their customers. We will take a closer look and see how the firms identify its major competitors and the way competing them.

Who are our competitors?

The term itself denotes that they are firms that provide the same business nature of others. In the case of a restaurant, his competitors are also a restaurant however; it differs in terms of size, capability and reliability. There are different types of competitor that the firm faces in their day-to-day operations and describing those leads the firm to find potential opportunity of their presence. Below enumerate some of them.
1. Immediate
2. Non-immediate
3. Potential

Immediate

The competition describe as firm offering identical product or services. The degree of competition is head-to-head considering that firms are catering the same kinds of customers. In the case of a restaurant business, the only way to prosper with immediate competition is making their product unique and creation of surprising menu to delight customers. Some world renowned food chain such as Jollibee, KFC, and McDonald are the closest competing food business. They are situated most likely in the same location giving customers an array of choice. The firms exist despite of the strong competition because they continuously create something new that enticed consumers to visit often. Immediate strong competition brings a meaningful advantage because business will keep on experimenting things and make continuous improvements.

Non-immediate

These firms are classified as carrying close substitutes products. This type of competitors cannot be underestimated considering that they will harm other business if opportunity warrants. The business nature is somewhat the same with immediate competitors for they tries to capture a marginal market share as the immediate competitors do.

Potential

These types of competitors does not bring an immediate or non-immediate effect to business however, they are the potential competitors as the years to come. A business is surrounded with different businesses in the environment. When you look at the surrounding and when your business is a restaurant, what you think of your competitors are the one that directly affect your business. However, those that are not directly affecting you would bring a slight impact to competition unnoticed

Consider a small sari-sari store that sells soft drink and .your restaurant sells the same too. A customer might prefer to drink in the sari-sari store rather than in your restaurant for unexplained reasons, little by little affects your sales by all means. Hence potential competitors are those that do not bring direct or indirect impact to business however; it can move to be a strong competitor in the future. Identifying who are your competitors can be best described using a model and this is shown below.

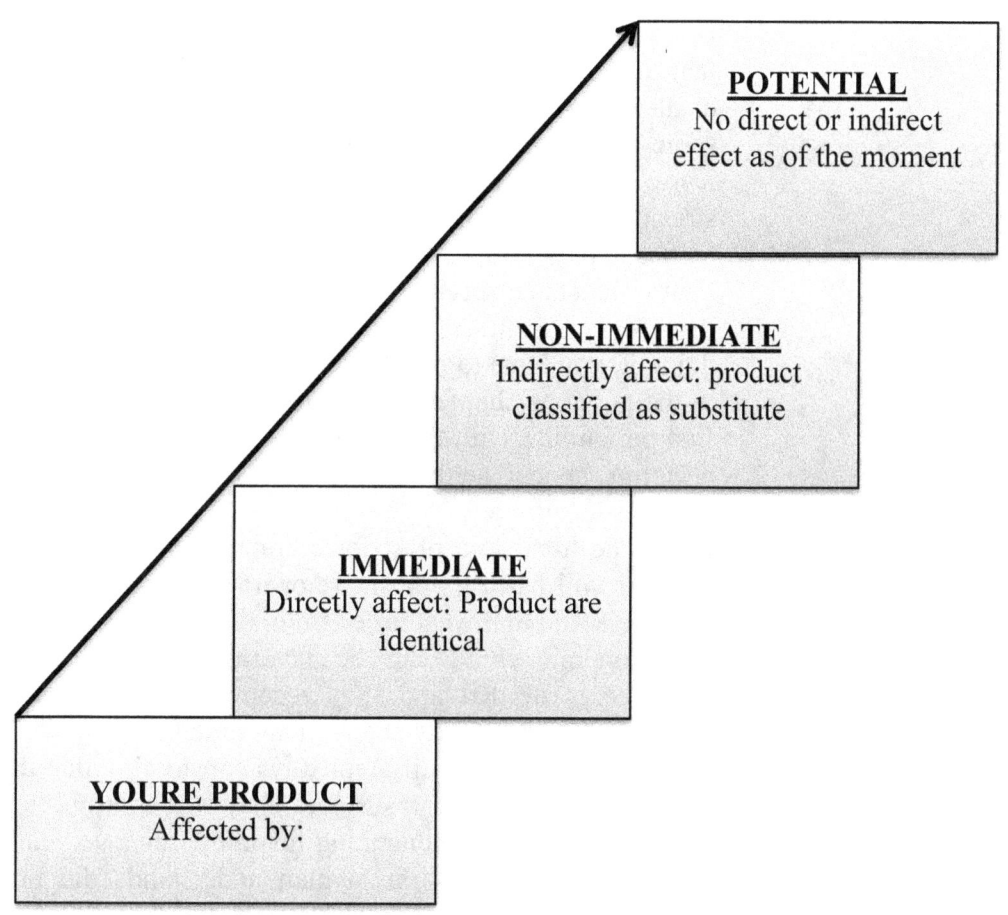

Figure 4 shows the ladder of product competition

The effective way of determining a successful competitive analysis is by knowing how your competitors behave and identifying strategy used and enables firms discover opportunity behind it.

SUMMARY

1. Industry analysis is vital to the firm for this will guide them how to counter competition. An effective industry analysis suggested that the firm should be guided with some business models to understand the value proposition and answer questions leading to finding realistic approach in problem solving such as (1) is the location ideal for the chosen business? This means that, are there potentials (the traffic, the environment, people, industry around that be pointed as customers, (2) is the firm ready to face challenge? (3) Is there a possibility that the firm will experience some unfavorable circumstances in the course of doing business? Knowing this is very important for business to position in a very strategic location for this will bring will bring them into a greater height if they will be able to maintain and sustain the quality of their product and services.
2. Business is like deciding to take a dive in the pool however; prior doing it, you have to check the deepness of it. As discussed earlier in the previous chapter, to be strong enough in business, we must first be familiar with the environment we are in and how business performs hence' studying the trends are very essential for the business to survive.
3. Economic trend is a must for entrepreneurs to know considering that this will harm the business operation by not getting aware of it. As it is said that what is certain in this world is change.
4. An economic trend can be favorable or unfavorable hence; vigilance is needed and it is recommended that an alternative course of action is ready at any given time.
5. Business competes in different ways considering that the firm will always find ways how to survive. They will continue searching for some possibilities of generating favorable revenue. Business trend is another factor that for layman understands did not bring an impact to business.
6. **Business tend is** another factor to consider in industry analysis for this will contribute unfavorable effect to business. Businesses are govern with certain rules and regulation implemented by the government. In the case of political trend, some business suffers

due to strong political interventions. The mall political practices discourage business owners due to unfair government practices.
7. Establishing any forms of business always face challenge regardless of its nature and capitalization. Small business such as an ordinary sari-sari store is not exempted to experience the same competition as large businesses do.
8. Competition is always there considering that all business enthusiast will always take advantage of gaining at least a marginal return of the amount invested.
9. The closer the product substitute to the main product is likely to create some chaos to them considering that the small difference wold triggers consumer to shift to product substitutes. On the hand, if the threat of substitute is not that strong, it would mean attractive to the main product.
10. The entry of a new firm in the industry brings favorable and unfavorable impressions to the business activity. A business without competition has a lesser chances of creating some improvements hence; entry of the new player becomes favorable for this will create an initiative to firm owners to make some improvement in many ways. On the other hand, this new entrants can bring unfavorable impact to the existing businesses if they are outweigh in terms of product offerings.
11. Economies of scale a process of creating and maximizing firm competitive advantage over the new entrants. The San Miguel Corporation a world renowned beer maker and has a centennial dominance in the market of beer created different product lines to position in different market segment. With this kind of strategy, the firm is not easily bothered with new firm entering in the industry because of the wide variety of product that are already positioned to different target market.
12. The economies of scale are firm's strategy that applies the activity of producing more products with a lesser cost. Large Corporation often experience the presence of the new entrant however; new players finds it hard to penetrate and capture their existing market share. Coca Cola, Pepsi and Nestle Corporation are among the large firm that is known to have practicing the economies of scale.
13. Product differentiation denotes keeping firm's product intensively unique from others. The concept of product differentiation is innovation. Innovation is a continuing process of creativity making a strong consumers patronage. In the Philippines for example and talking about cell phones, there are variety of brands and models.

In order for the product to be differentiated, firms create some feature of it not found to some other competing products. This is done by the firm not only to keep their existing customers and capture nee ones but to block competitors.

14. Rivalry is inevitable as it is always the bottom line of every business. Rivalry affects some business alike up to the extent of price wars. Price war is not a healthy competition practice for business however; due to the presence of close substitute products, firm tend to reduce price and lowers down their percentage of revenue. Products where competition is not that intense would likely to earn more than product with closed substitutes.

15. Close substitute's means that in the absence of the main product gives assurance to the substitute product as buyer's preference. Observing the market today and considering that there are lot of product with close substitutes, cell phones for example, dealers cannot make a bigger mark-up for the item because of many available dealers that sells identical product. Their ultimate strategy is to sell more units despite of lesser percentage of mark-up, at the end of the day, the volume of unit sold accounts for a bigger profit.

16. The presence of more competitors in similar market is more likely that one or more will initiate to lower down their price to attract buyers. Although the practice itself is not recommended however; for the business to survive, some strategy should be initiated by the firm. Common practices by firms in similar market use the so-called "fast moving product, reduced price". This means that firms observes which product is frequently purchased by buyers, then firms reduces its price to create an impression that he's price is low compared to others. This is one of the strategies that most competing firms are doing but other commodity is priced beyond normal. Accounting this strategy, the firm still earns and keep their loyal buyers.

17. Competitors are major elements that affect every business towards achieving goals hence it is very important for the firm to analyse and understand the direction and identify market with which to compete. Competitor analysis is a detailed flat form that defines the degree of competition. It guides the firm in identifying some effective ways of knowing the positions of their competitors and from then, finding how to gain competitive advantage. This is very important aspect especially to those new ventures entering into a very competitive nature of business

DISUCUSSION QUESTIONS

1. Why is competitor analysis a requirement for every firm? Is by doing this a guarantee in business success? If so, discuss why?
2. Discuss some favorable and unfavorable impacts of competitor analysis to the firm.
3. Discuss the elements of economic trend and how do they help in the attainment of the firm's goals?
4. In what way do political trends affect business operations? Discuss.
5. In what instance a business trend helps the firm in finding other opportunities? Discuss.
6. At what degree do political trends affect the business especially to the start-ups ? Discuss.
7. Why do firms need to identify threats? It is said that these are opportunities. How do you reconcile this statement? Discuss.
8. Discuss the role of product substitute. What specific area does this affect the main product? Discuss.
9. Name some of the factors that cause other firms to feel threatened to new business entrants? Discuss.
10. What is product differentiation? What make products different? Discuss.
11. Discuss the elements that are contributed by firm's rivalry.
12. How are suppliers affected by bargaining power of buyers? Discuss the way they are influenced.
13. Discuss some measures the firm should do in order not to be affected by competition.
14. What are the ways of classifying competitors and how should the firm overcome them? Discuss.

KEY TERMS (According to their appearance)

competitors analysis	**social responsibility**	**business**
models	**economic trends**	**capitalization**
business enthusiast	**substitutes**	**bargaining**
power	**differentiation**	**blocking**
force	**economies of scale**	**rivalry degree**
of competition	**degree of differentiation**	**cost standing**

Works Cited

1. Alcacer, J. (2001). Strategy and geography the impact of firm rivalry on location choices in global high tech industries.
2. Bodie, Z., Kane, A., & Marcus, A. J. (2011). Investments. New York: McGraw-Hill/Irwin. Competition. (2004). New York: United Nations.
3. Ding, H. (2013). Three Essays on Buyer Power, Market Structure and Government Subsidies.
4. Haney, L. H. (1922). The business trend - A barometer of industry and trade .. New York: The Ronald Press.
5. Hayek, F. A., Bartley, W. W., & Kresge, S. (1991). *The trend of economic thinking: Essays on political economists and economic history*. Chicago: University of Chicago Press.
6. Kuroda, A. (2000). *Recent China's economy and trend of industries. Part 1: Economic trend*. Tokyo.

INTERNET SITE ADDRESSES

For the list of definitions of competitor analysis, see

1. phttps://www.google.com.

2. https://www.google.com.

CHAPTER 8

PUTTING THINGS TOGETHER
(Designing a Business of Your Own)

Introduction

Designing one's business entails a long process in which this book has discussed thoroughly from the beginning to this part. This chapter finally conjoins all the factors and processes that greatly affect any real business. These factors include the product concept, business planning, the entrepreneurial growth and management, developing a market research and the industry competitor analysis and social responsibility. A real business suggests having clear fundamentals; hence, adoption of a business model canvas will help a lot to new business start-up such as the model designed by U.C Berkeley in a start-up competition. The following elements serve as guide on how to go about real business concept:

- The value proposition
- Customer Relationships
- Customer segments
- Channels
- Key resources
- Key activities
- Key partners
- Cost structure
- Revenue stream

DEFINITION OF TERMS

The value proposition is referred to as the main product and services of the firm intended for their customers. The product is designed to answer the need of the target consumers.

Customer relationship is a process of understanding and evaluating customer's needs through a consistent communication and developing business relationships. Developing customer relationships can be achieved by assisting them on what they want, how they want it and when they want it.

Customer segment is an act of breaking down the market into a smaller unit or groups of consumers and designs a specific strategy for that segment.

Channels mean transferring of goods and services to identified groups of consumers. A channel can be of different ways; using people to people, transportation and the like.

Key resources refer to the most important elements in making a business such as machineries and equipment. It can also be referred to manpower resources or people that possess the necessary skills needed to run the business. The key resources help in building firms a good value proposition that help them in generating revenue.

Key activities refer to the major task the company engages in. The key activity varies depending on what the firm wants to do in the business.

Key partners are the key players in the business. They represent as the major components that contribute to business success.

Cost structure is involved in determining the incurred cost using the fixed and variable materials in running the business.

Revenue stream is the amount of money generated out of doing business. It is a detailed summary that shows how business makes money from the resources used.

THE BUSINESS AND ITS APPLICATIONS

Business application is a very important element in the entrepreneurial point of view considering that the study will clearly apply the methods on how to effectively draw a business upon achieving its desired revenue margins. A good business application should define the elements found in the business model canvas and effectively answer the following guide questions enumerated below:

Key Partners: This identifies your business partners by answering the following questions:
Who are your key partners?
Who are your key suppliers?
What key resources are you acquiring from partners?
What key activities do your partners perform?

Key Activities are the major activities to be done in the business. These tasks can easily be answered by focusing on the given questions:
What key activities does your value proposition require?
Customer Relationships?
Revenue stream?

Value Proposition defines what products are made for customer's needs. Defining them requires answering the given questions:
What value do you deliver to the customer?
Which one of your customer's problems are you helping to solve?
What type of product and services are you offering to each customer segment?
Which customer's needs are you satisfying?

Customer Relationships identify how the firm establishes relationships to customers. Guiding them ideally by answering the following questions:
What type of relationships do you have for each of your customers?
Does the segment expect you to establish and maintain with them?
Which one have you established?
How are they integrated with the rest of your business models?
How costly are they?

Customer Segment identifies what segment or customer is being served and doing this can be easy by answering these questions.
For whom are you doing a value?
Who are your most important customers?

Cost structure is the most critical part to be considered in doing business for it will affect the revenue of the firm; hence, it is important to identify them and answer the following guide questions.
What are the most important costs inherent to the business model?
Which resources are most expensive?
Which key activity is most expensive?

Revenue Streams is the method of understanding the behaviour of customers in terms paying habit. This can be easy by answering the guide questions.
For what value are your customers really willing to pay?
For what our customers do currently pay?
How are they currently paying?
How would they prefer to pay?
How much amount of overall revenue the stream contributed?

On this part, defining and summarizing the elements found in the business model canvas are done. The next step is designing an actual business structure guided by the model. In the previous chapters, mineral water business was cited and now a product model to be used for a real business application.

THE BUSINESS ENVIRONMENT

Business is embraced with different types of barriers and what is common to all is competition. The activity is referred to a situation where firms try to gain advantage over others by defeating them with an attempt to gain superiority to the activity. A business practice can be best achieved by identifying the guide provided by the business model canvas. Let's start by identifying what type of product we want to engage in. Consider a business of mineral water and let us examine how to do it using the model. The first approach is putting some information to the value proposition. See the steps shown below.

1. **Value Proposition**
    1.1 Quality mineral water
    1.2 Shortage of safe water
    1.3 Different sizes of bottled water
    1.4 Satisfy their thirst with safe water

2. **Customer Segment**
    2.1 All customer levels
    2.2 All water users

3. **Channels**
    3.1 Direct distribution
    3.2 Distributorship

4. **Customer Relationship**
    4.1 Customer-consumers
    4.2 Wholesale and retail segment

5. **Key partners**
    5.1 Container provider
    5.2 Manpower
    5.3 Trackers
    5.4 Storage

6. Key Activity
   6.1 Processing
   6.2 Bottling
   6.3 Labelling
   6.4 Distributing

7. Key Resources
   7.1 Manpower
   7.2 Capital

8. Cost Structure
   8.1 Distribution
   8.2 Equipment

9. Revenue Stream
   9.1 Cash on delivery
   9.2 Term payment
   9.3 80 percent revenue

The above detailed information can be derived by using the enumerated details of the activity so that the firm can easily determine the possible cost incurred in coming up a business. The above illustrative approach can be better understood if supported with a business feasibility study.

FEASIBILITY ANALYSIS AND PROCEDURES

Business endeavour is subject to success and failures depending on how the firm designs its activity towards achieving business's goals efficiently. A good planning that defines clear direction can lead to a potential business advantage. Most firms rely much of having a feasibility study to guide them in venturing business efforts. A feasibility study helps in assessing the practicability of the proposed plan. It analyses the business if it is feasible to ensure that profitability is realistic considering that it involves large sum of money. There are four key elements comprising the conduct of doing a feasibility study as shown below.
   1. Product feasibility
   2. Market feasibility
   3. Organizational feasibility
   4. Financial feasibility

Product feasibility

Product feasibility is very important among all involved in the study as product represents the real image of the company. The revenue desired by firm can be impossible if the product does not have an applauding market acceptance. The objective of product feasibility study covers two elements such as product *desirability* and the *demand*. The product desirability is done by firms to affirm that in the event product is launched it will have a meaningful acceptance in the market place. The determination of market demand for a certain product is the real essence of feasibility study whenever information doesn't warrant, efforts could be useless. On the other hand, product desirability plays a vital role considering that this will help the firm in terms of determining the customer's preferences. The product is in danger with its situation even its availability is feasible but the buyers' preference is not on the firm's product could result to business discomforts. Product feasibility can be effective if the firm tries to assess by answering questions by themselves such as:

- ✓ Are we creating product that answer the immediate need of consumers and providing them the goods that will surely excite them?
- ✓ Does it provide solution to gap problems and bring to the firm competitive advantage?
- ✓ Is the plan of introducing the product in the market timely considering environment and social changes?
- ✓ Is there a strong competition between the characteristics and design of the product that arouse the buyer's interest?

The general objective why a firm needs to have a feasibility study is to gather vital information for the proposed plan upon knowing the presence of potential demand in the market and finally make a conclusion out of it. A test called concept testing applies for it which describes the product in the following areas such as:

1. Product features
2. Consumers
3. Product benefits
4. Product positioning
5. The company

Example of concept testing survey affirming the buyer's response statement

<u>Guide questions</u>

1. What do you like most of the product and services described in this survey?
2. Can you provide suggestions that will somehow improve the product and services farther?
3. How do you assess the idea in terms of its feasibility?
4. What possible suggestions can you give to best help improve the product and services described in this survey?
5. What recommendation can you provide for product features to increase customer's preferences?

Figure 1 shows an example of concept testing survey affirming buyer's response statement.

Example survey sheets (buyer's intentions)

<u>Guide questions</u>

1. How frequent will you buy our product and services, if it will be available in the market?
   ___ Always
   ___ Almost always
   ___ Sometimes
   ___ Most of the times
   ___ Never
   ___ undecided

Figure 2 shows the buyer's survey responses

Market feasibility

It is an assessment of the total product made by different firms in the market by prospect buyers. There are underlying elements that separate the understanding between industry and buyers that need to be clarified. *Industry* per se, refers to firms or group of firms that produces identical products. Their *target market* is confined within their desired scope considering that it is not that easy to position their products in a wider scope. The most common practices of the firm as they begin are to start in one specific target area and to gradually expand as product acceptance increases and revenue commensurate investment. There are two elements that embrace the effort of conducting the market feasibility which describes *how attractive is the industry* and *how attractive is the target market*. These two cited elements can be best understood using a diagram shown below on figure3.

Description of Attractive industry
✓ Modern and reliable
✓ Advance and technical
✓ Fragmented rather than focused
✓ Inclining rather than declining
✓ Focus on need rather than wants
✓ Spacious ambiance
✓ Profitable
✓ Business independence

Figure 3 shows the description of attractive industry

The above industry description is very essential in the present times as environment changes. Buyers nowadays are becoming more meticulous in choosing types of industry they prefer. The above enumerated descriptions of an attractive industry rhyme with the desire of almost majority of the consumers alike. On the other hand, the target market attractiveness is usually referred to as having the potential in doing business. There are some elements that qualify a market to be attractive such as presence of large market segment which means more buyers, a lot of segments to venture with and favorable to those new start-ups. More favorable circumstances can be found in an attractive target market making most firms prioritize serving them.

Organizational feasibility

It is very essential for management to conduct an organizational feasibility leading towards *determining available members having the capacity and skills needed, available resources and the overall management competences.* The proposed launching of business could be in chaotic situation in the absence of these basic elements. The key major components noted to be very important in the organization's feasibility efforts is to deepen understanding regarding *"management ability"*, and *"sufficiency of resources"* needed for the venture. The importance of these major components is discussed further to emphasize their crucial contribution to the proposed business.

Management ability

Success of the business endeavour lies largely on how the management perceives the possibilities of getting into the market which calls for their total readiness. Management ability requirement applies to all types of business whether a sole owner or a corporation. Every business aims at getting some benefits in doing business; hence, the most important requirement for making success is commitment and passion to reach goals. Understanding the market that the firm will venture requires sustaining strength for there is no substitute to it.

Resources availability

Resources are another components that help in attaining organization's goal. The management should consider that by obtaining them does not require an amount of time, rather the resources must be sufficient so the firm can easily move forward in doing business. Resources do not only limit to equipment but most importantly are the people. It said that in modern times technology changes some business images. This holds true to many businesses today but nothing replaces people as the most important resources. Resources feasibility is most likely focused on nonfinancial such as the skills where firms should look into among the pool of employees. An employee can be a good one but the skills are somewhat more difficult to find which are not present to all employees. To ensure that the firm is ready for the venture, it is suggested that they should identify some critical nonfinancial resources that hamper firms' operation if not defined well. Some examples of nonfinancial resources are however critical to operation as shown in table below.

Table of nonfinancial resources affecting business operations

> ✓ Affordable production areas (Production space)
> ✓ Key partners (this can be suppliers or skilled people)
> ✓ Support people (Other team members)
> ✓ Operational equipment (Machine and equipment)
> ✓ Legal requirements
> ✓ Key management

Figure 4 shows the elements of nonfinancial resources

Financial feasibility

It is the final stage of the feasibility analysis that concentrates on the financial capacity of the firm. This is done to assess firm's financial strength and to ascertain its capability to sustain the operation. Analysing financial capacity of the firm does not only limit on accounting how much financial resource available when needed however, this includes sourcing out if in the event the call for a need is urgent. A good standing firm does not face some financial constraints for it can make an arrangement to identify a financial institution for support. Financial feasibility can be beneficial for every firm if they are acquainted on the business operations and able to assess and answer some questions related to their operations like: how much is invested, what is the degree of risk faced in doing the business venture?, what are some outlets for financial reinvestment for some retained earnings?, and what are some ways that may help the venture?.

SUMMARY

1. The business making is not that easy. The new ventures must be guided by some business strategies such as the value proposition, customer relations, customer segments, channels, key resources, key partners, activities, resources, and revenue structure. Understanding the nine elements helps the firm and the new ventures make a clear definition of the activity and its processess.
2. The value proposition is referred to as the main product and services of the firm intended for their customers. The product is designed to answer the needs of the target consumers.
3. Customer relationship is a process of understanding and evaluating customer's needs through a consistent communication and developing business relationships. Developing customer

relationships can be achieved by assisting them what they want, how they want it and when they want it.

4. Business application is a very important element in the entrepreneurial point of view considering that the study will clearly apply the methods on how to effectively draw a business that assures its desired revenue margins.

5. A good business application should define the elements found in the business model canvas and effectively answer the following guide questions.

6. Cost structure is the most critical part to be considered in doing business for this will affect the revenue of the firm hence, it is important to identify them and answer the following guide questions such as: What are the most important costs inherent to the business model? Which resources are most expensive? and Which key activity is most expensive?

7. Business is embraced with different types of barriers and what is common to all is competition. The activity is referred to a situation where firms try to gain advantage over others. By defeating others is an attempt to gain superiority to the activity.

8. Business endeavour is subject to success and failures depending on how the firm designs its activity towards achieving business goals efficiently. A good planning that defines clear direction can lead to a potential business advantage. Most firms rely much of having a feasibility study to guide them in venturing business efforts. A feasibility study helps in assessing the practicability of the proposed plan. It analyses the business if it is feasible to ensure that profitability is realistic considering that it involves large sum of money.

9. Product feasibility is very important among all involved in the study as product represents the real image of the company. The revenue desired by the firm can be impossible if the product does not have an applauding market acceptance. The objective of product feasibility study covers two elements such as product *desirability* and the *demand*.

10. The product desirability is done by firms to affirm that in the event a product is launched it will have a meaningful acceptance in the market place. To determine the demand for a certain product in the market is the real essence of feasibility study whenever information doesn't warrant, efforts could be useless. On the other hand, product desirability plays a vital role considering that this will help the firm in terms of determining

the customer preferences. The product is in danger with its situation even its availability is feasible but once the buyer's preference is not on the firms product, it could result to business discomforts

11. The general objective why firm needs to have a feasibility study is to gather vital information for the proposed plan and know the presence of potential demand in the market for their proposed venture and finally make a conclusion out of it.

12. Market feasibility assesses the total product produced by different firms in the market by prospect buyers. There are underlying elements that separate the understanding between industry and buyers that need to be clarified. *Industry* per se, refers to firms or group of firms that produces identical products.

13. The *target market* is confined within their desired scope considering that it is not that easy to position the product in a wider scope. The most common practices of the firm as they begin are to start in one specific target area and to gradually expand as product acceptance increases and the revenue commensurate investment. There are two elements that embrace the effort of conducting the market feasibility which describe *how attractive is the industry* and *how attractive is the target market*.

14. Organizational feasibility is very essential for the management to conduct for it leads towards determining available members having the capacity and skills needed, available resources and the overall management competences.

15. The proposed launching of business could be in a chaotic situation in the absence of these basic elements. The key major components noted to be very important in the organization's feasibility efforts are to deepen the understanding regarding *"management ability"*, and *"sufficiency of resources"* needed for the venture. The importance of these major components is discussed further to emphasize their crucial contribution to the proposed business.

16. Success of the business endeavour lies largely on how the management perceives the possibilities of getting into the market which calls for their total readiness. Management ability requirement applies to all types of business whether a sole owner or a corporation. Every business aims at getting some benefits in doing business; hence, the most important requirements to reach a goal are commitment and passion. Understanding the market

that the firm will participate in requires a sustained strength for no practical substitutes of it.

17. Resources are other components that help in attaining organization's goal that management should consider which does not require an amount of time. Sufficient resources can easily make a firm move forward in doing business.
18. Resources do not only limit to equipment but the most important resource are people. It said that in modern times technology changes some business images. This holds true to many businesses today but nothing replaces people as the important resources.
19. Resources feasibility is most likely focused on non-financial such as the skills of each employee in which firms should look into. An employee can be a good one but he may lack the skills the company needs or his skills are not found among others. To ensure that the firm is ready for the venture, it is suggested that they should identify some critical non-financial resources that may hamper firm's operation if not defined well.
20. Financial feasibility is the final stage of the feasibility analysis that concentrates on the financial capacity of the firm. This is done to assess firm's financial strength and to ascertain its capability to sustain the operation. Analysing financial capacity of the firm does not only limit on accounting how much financial resource available when needed but it includes sourcing out once the call for a need is urgent.

DISCUSSION QUESTIONS

==

1. Why is understanding the value proposition a prerequisite for the firm prior to its business venture? Discuss.
2. Business is dependent on its customers as they patronize its products. Why does a firm need to study consumer's behavior and how does it affect the business? Discuss.
3. Segmentation is a tool in marketing. What is the contribution of a good segmentation to firms? Discuss.
4. Discuss how important is channel. Why does this remain a problem to the firm despite the advent of technology?
5. Discuss the elements found in the business model canvas and enumerate some of their benefits when used in business.

6. Who are the key partners in business? Discuss their roles and contributions to business ventures' success.
7. How important is revenue to the firm? Enumerate and discuss some ways that help in realizing them.
8. Business is known to have embraced different barriers. As a businessman, what are the possible barriers you may encounter and how will you overcome them?
9. It is a common practice for business that in order to prosper, they need to have feasibility study. If this is so, why do some businesses fail? Discuss.
10. In product feasibility, discuss how demand and desirability contribute to business.
11. Why do firms need to know the buyer's intentions? How important is conducting a survey to determine customer's intentions despite its expense? Discuss.
12. In market feasibility, discuss the underlying elements that separate industry and buyers.

KEY Terms (In order of their appearance)

Business models	**cost structure**	**revenue stream**
value proposition	**customer segments**	**feasibility business**
venture	**product desirability**	**resource sufficiency**

Works Cited

1. Cartwright, Roger. *Customer Relationships*. Oxford: Capstone, 2003. Print.
2. Cheverton, Peter. *Key Marketing Skills: Strategies, Tools, and Techniques for Marketing Success*. London: Kogan Page, 2004. Print.
3. Egelman, Edward H., and Mauricio Montal. *Channels*. Amsterdam: Elsevier, 2012. Print.
4. Gordon, Ian. *Managing the New Customer Relationship: Strategies to Engage the Social Customer and Build Lasting Value*. Mississauga, Ont.: J. Wiley & Sons Canada, 2013. Print.
5. Hughes, Arthur Middleton. *The Customer Loyalty Solution: What Works (and What Doesn't) in Customer Loyalty Programs*. New York: McGraw-Hill, 2003. Print.

6. Katz, Helen E. *The Media Handbook: A Complete Guide to Advertising Media Selection, Planning, Research, and Buying.* Mahwah, NJ: L. Erlbaum Associates, 2007. Print.
7. *Revenue Stream: An Economic Analysis of the Costs and Benefits of Removing the Four Dams on the Lower Snake River.* Place of Publication Not Identified: Taxpayers for Common Sense, 2006. Print.
8. Stephens, Chris S., and Jenny Sullivan. *Activities Based on Siôn and the Bargain Bee by Jenny Sullivan.* Cardiff: WJEC, 2002. Print.

www.ingramcontent.com/pod-product-compliance
Lightning Source LLC
Chambersburg PA
CBHW081151180526

45170CB00006B/2028